THE UNITED STATES, CHINA,
AND ARMS CONTROL

THE UNITED STATES, CHINA, AND ARMS CONTROL

Ralph N. Clough
A. Doak Barnett
Morton H. Halperin
Jerome H. Kahan
with Alton H. Quanbeck and Barry M. Blechman

The Brookings Institution
Washington, D.C.

Copyright © 1975 by
THE BROOKINGS INSTITUTION
1775 Massachusetts Avenue, N.W., Washington, D.C. 20036

Library of Congress Cataloging in Publication Data:

Main entry under title:

The United States, China, and arms control.

  Bibliography: p.
  Includes index.
1. Atomic weapons and disarmament.
2. China–Defenses.
3. United States–Defenses.
 i. Clough, Ralph N., 1916–
ii. Brookings Institution, Washington, D.C.

JX1974.7.U63   327′.174   75-15650
ISBN 0-8157-1478-5
ISBN 0-8157-1477-7 pbk.

9 8 7 6 5 4 3 2 1

THE BROOKINGS INSTITUTION is an independent organization devoted to nonpartisan research, education, and publication in economics, government, foreign policy, and the social sciences generally. Its principal purposes are to aid in the development of sound public policies and to promote public understanding of issues of national importance.

The Institution was founded on December 8, 1927, to merge the activities of the Institute for Government Research, founded in 1916, the Institute of Economics, founded in 1922, and the Robert Brookings Graduate School of Economics and Government, founded in 1924.

The Board of Trustees is responsible for the general administration of the Institution, while the immediate direction of the policies, program, and staff is vested in the President, assisted by an advisory committee of the officers and staff. The by-laws of the Institution state: "It is the function of the Trustees to make possible the conduct of scientific research, and publication, under the most favorable conditions, and to safeguard the independence of the research staff in the pursuit of their studies and in the publication of the results of such studies. It is not a part of their function to determine, control, or influence the conduct of particular investigations or the conclusions reached."

The President bears final responsibility for the decision to publish a manuscript as a Brookings book. In reaching his judgment on the competence, accuracy, and objectivity of each study, the President is advised by the director of the appropriate research program and weighs the views of a panel of expert outside readers who report to him in confidence on the quality of the work. Publication of a work signifies that it is deemed a competent treatment worthy of public consideration but does not imply endorsement of conclusions or recommendations.

The Institution maintains its position of neutrality on issues of public policy in order to safeguard the intellectual freedom of the staff. Hence interpretations or conclusions in Brookings publications should be understood to be solely those of the authors and should not be attributed to the Institution, to its trustees, officers, or other staff members, or to the organizations that support its research.

Foreword

Since the detonation of its first nuclear explosive device in 1964, the People's Republic of China has constructed a strategic nuclear force that in 1974 may have consisted of as many as eighty medium-range and intermediate-range missiles and a hundred jet-powered medium bombers capable of striking targets in neighboring Asian countries and the USSR. The Chinese are continuing to work on intercontinental ballistic missiles, and by the 1980s they may have missiles that can reach cities on this continent. The United States thus faces a new strategic situation and a new arms control problem.

The authors of this study consider whether Chinese nuclear weaponry is likely to affect the U.S.–Soviet strategic balance and analyze the possible influence of such weaponry on U.S. policies toward Japan and other East Asian countries. They examine Chinese attitudes toward arms control and outline a variety of possible approaches to agreements with China on arms control measures. They particularly emphasize the prospects for U.S.–Chinese negotiations focused on two proposals—reciprocal pledges by each nation not to be the first to use nuclear weapons against the other and international agreements concerning the Korean peninsula, including the establishment of a nuclear-free zone. In the author's view, the United States should, in its own interest, seek to involve China soon in bilateral private or official discussions on arms control.

At the time when the study on which this book is based was carried out, all the authors were Brookings senior fellows. Two are still on the Brookings staff: Ralph Clough, former director of the State Department's Office of Chinese Affairs and a former member of its Policy Planning Council, and A. Doak Barnett, author of numerous books on China and student of Chinese affairs for more than twenty-five years.

Morton H. Halperin, formerly Deputy Assistant Secretary of Defense for International Affairs and senior staff member of the National Security Council, left Brookings in 1973 to undertake a study under the auspices of the Twentieth Century Fund. Jerome H. Kahan, a former official of the Department of Defense and of the Arms Control and Disarmament Agency, joined the Policy Planning Staff of the Department of State in 1974.

The authors thank Alton H. Quanbeck and Barry M. Blechman, both Brookings senior fellows and members of the defense analysis staff of the Brookings Foreign Policy Studies program, for preparing the appendix and for their advice on the entire manuscript. The manuscript was edited by Ellen A. Ash; the index was prepared by Helen B. Eisenhart.

This study is based on research conducted under a contract between the Arms Control and Disarmament Agency and the Brookings Institution. The authors are grateful for the cooperation of officials of that agency and other departments of the federal government, as well as for the advice and comments of private American specialists in Chinese affairs.

The views expressed here are those of the authors and should not be ascribed to the U.S. Arms Control and Disarmament Agency, to any other department or agency of the U.S. government, or to other persons and organizations consulted in the preparation of the study. Nor should they be ascribed to the trustees, officers, or other staff members of the Brookings Institution.

KERMIT GORDON
President

April 1975
Washington, D.C.

Contents

THE UNITED STATES, CHINA,
AND ARMS CONTROL

Introduction

Before the end of the 1970s the People's Republic of China (PRC) will have deployed a small but significant strategic nuclear force. In 1974 this force probably consisted of as many as 70–80 medium-range and intermediate-range ballistic missiles (MRBMs and IRBMs)[1] and 100 jet-powered medium bombers capable of reaching targets in Asia and the USSR. By the 1980s this force could be supplemented by intercontinental ballistic missiles (ICBMs) with a range long enough to reach cities in the United States. Although this Chinese nuclear force will be far inferior to those of the United States and the Soviet Union, both superpowers will have to consider seriously its implications in formulating their strategic and arms control policies.

The rapid movement of events in international politics in the past few years has rendered out of date appraisals made as recently as three or four years ago of the implications of the Chinese nuclear force for the United States. The tension between China and the Soviet Union, the improvement of relations between Peking and Washington, the signing of the Strategic Arms Limitation Talks (SALT) agreements by the United States and the USSR, developments in Vietnam, and the resurgence of Japan all require a new look at the Chinese nuclear force and its implications for U.S. policy.

The authors of this study endorse the rapprochement with China, the withdrawal of U.S. combat forces from Vietnam, the reversion of Okinawa to Japan, and, in general, the effort to shift to U.S. allies greater

---

1. The three categories of strategic nuclear ballistic missiles are differentiated by range. MRBMs have a range from 600 to 1,500 miles; IRBMs from 1,500 to 3,000 miles; and ICBMs over 3,000 miles. For a detailed estimate of China's future nuclear force see Appendix.

responsibility for their own defense and to define more narrowly the contingencies in which the United States would consider intervening with its own forces. The authors place great emphasis on the importance to peace and stability in Asia of Japan's remaining a lightly armed, nonnuclear power, and the consequent need to give high priority in U.S. policy to maintaining a healthy U.S.–Japanese alliance. The authors assign a relatively low value to U.S. security interests in Southeast Asia and, therefore, see a low risk in the complete withdrawal of U.S. combat forces from mainland Southeast Asia despite the probable repercussions of the victory of North Vietnamese and Kmer Rouge forces in South Vietnam and Cambodia.[2] The authors also question in certain respects the design of U.S. forces maintained to deter China.

The evaluation of the implications of China's nuclear force for the United States is based on certain premises: (1) that proliferation of nuclear weapons is not in the U.S. interest; (2) that a continuing close and cooperative relationship with Japan is essential to peace in East Asia; (3) that it is important to U.S. interests to continue improving relations with China; (4) that strategic stability with the Soviet Union is a basic requirement for peace; (5) that U.S. interests are better served by relative stability in international relations, characterized by gradual, peaceful change, than by an unstable, highly unpredictable international environment; and (6) that it is better for nuclear powers to talk to each other about arms control than not to talk, even though agreement might not be possible for a long time. The authors have not attempted to justify these basic premises here, for to do so would require a discussion ranging far beyond the scope of this study.

The nuclear force that China can be expected to possess within the next five to ten years raises a number of questions, which this study addresses. Some have broad political significance. What effect will the Chinese nuclear force have on the credibility of the defense commitments of the United States to its allies, on nuclear proliferation, and on the prospects for achieving the objectives of the United States in East Asia? Other questions are primarily military. Will the existence of the Chinese nuclear force compel the United States to add to its strategic nuclear weapons, either offensive or defensive? Will it affect the stra-

2. The rationale behind these views has been set out in other Brookings studies: Henry Owen (ed.), *The Next Phase in Foreign Policy* (1973); Ralph N. Clough, *East Asia and U.S. Security* (1975); and A. Doak Barnett, *Uncertain Passage: China's Transition to the Post-Mao Era* (1974).

tegic balance between the United States and the USSR? Is it likely to make the Chinese more aggressive militarily, and hence to affect the level and deployment of U.S. general purpose forces?

China's nuclear force also raises critical questions about arms control. Should the United States seek to draw China into future SALT negotiations? What are the prospects for China's adhering to existing multilateral arms control agreements? Would Chinese nonadherence severely impair the effectiveness of such agreements? What types of future arms control negotiations might China be interested in, and what types would the Chinese probably oppose? Is it in the interest of the United States to try to draw China into a dialogue on arms control at an early date? What bilateral arms control arrangement between Washington and Peking might be practicable?

This study begins with an analysis of the role of nuclear weapons in Chinese foreign policy. The implications of the Chinese nuclear force for U.S. defense policy and for multilateral arms control are then discussed. Finally, possible U.S. approaches to arms control arrangements with China are outlined, and two are discussed in detail: a limited no-first-use (NFU) agreement with China and a nuclear-free zone (NFZ) in Korea.

The evolution of Chinese positions on nuclear weapons and arms control is not reviewed in this study. That has been done elsewhere, and the recent fundamental changes in the international political scene suggest the possibility of further significant modifications of Chinese positions during the next few years. This study attempts instead to reach judgments on how the leaders of China are likely to view the international scene in the years immediately ahead and, on that basis, to evaluate the implications for the United States of the Chinese nuclear force. The principal aim of the study is to identify the specific U.S. actions toward or agreements with China that offer the best promise both of improving relations between the United States and China and of involving the Chinese in serious negotiations on arms control measures without prejudicing the security of the United States or its relations with its allies.

Finally, the reader will note that in attempting to predict how China is likely to behave in the future the study has, for the most part, used the "single actor" model of political analysis. The authors have put forward hypotheses concerning Chinese behavior in various future situations on the basis of China's past policies, the declared objectives of

Chinese leaders, and the means likely to be at their disposal in relation to the means available to the other big powers. The assumption is that any Chinese leaders, *in matters affecting the security of their nation,* will behave prudently and rationally within the limits imposed by their world view, as they indeed appear to have done for the past twenty years.

One could, of course, imagine exigencies of domestic politics, for example in the course of a struggle for the succession to Mao Tse-tung, that might cause a Chinese leader to depart from a prudent and rational course in international affairs. But the lack of reliable data on the strength and functioning of domestic political forces and alignments in China makes it doubtful that a prediction based on an attempt to analyze bureaucratic politics in China would successfully forecast such an aberration. Hence, it appeared preferable for the purposes of this study to use the single actor model—recognizing the weaknesses of all such predictions—rather than to engage in a much more complex attempt to analyze internal politics in China with little prospect of more reliable results.

CHAPTER ONE

The Role of Nuclear Weapons in Chinese Foreign Policy

In analyzing China's foreign policy, and especially the propensity of the Chinese to use military force, it is essential to distinguish between Peking's strategic view and its tactical view. Confusing the two can lead the observer to make serious misjudgments and erroneous predictions.

"Despise the enemy strategically," says Mao Tse-tung, "but respect him tactically." When the *Peoples Daily* or *Red Flag* hails the "excellent revolutionary situation in the world today" and predicts the ultimate victory of "people's war," these are strategic assessments, indicating that Chinese leaders have confidence that there are broad trends in the world moving in what they believe to be the right direction, but they give no reliable clues as to Peking's next tactical moves. When, on the other hand, Chou En-lai or Teng Hsiao-p'ing discusses world politics with foreign visitors, although he may also speak from a conviction that long-term trends are moving the world irresistibly in the direction pointed out by Marxism-Leninism-Maoism, his remarks are likely to have a higher tactical content than articles in official publications. They will be relatively free of revolutionary jargon, sometimes refer explicitly to China's present tactical weakness, and often address directly immediate problems of Chinese foreign policy. Thus, an assessment of the role of nuclear weapons in China's foreign policy during the 1970s must take as a starting point the strategic viewpoint of Chinese leaders, with the recognition that over this rather short period specific actions may be determined more by tactical considerations than by long-term strategy.

The Strategic View

The attitudes of the Chinese toward other countries spring from their innate feeling that China is destined to become a world power with enormous influence. That there is no other country comparable to China in size or the length of history as a political entity gives the Chinese confidence that the sheer weight of China will inevitably make itself felt in the world. Chinese leaders thus feel that they need not be in a hurry to act or make concessions on matters they regard as matters of principle—they can afford to wait. As representatives of a great power they can be tough and unyielding or magnanimous as the case requires. But they will insist on being dealt with as equals by representatives of other great powers.

The present leaders of China used Marxism-Leninism, modified by Mao to suit Chinese conditions, as an instrument to gain power and to unify China under their leadership. It proved highly successful, and there is little reason to believe that they do not retain firm faith in its basic principles, as applicable both to China and to the world. Because these principles are general, they permit great flexibility in application. Those in power can rationalize in terms of Marxist-Leninist-Maoist philosophy anything they consider necessary to retain their power or to further China's national interests. Yet the leaders' commitment to this political philosophy inevitably influences the view they take of the world and limits the range of actions they would consider. Some Chinese leaders are doubtless more strongly influenced by ideological considerations than others, but all must be affected to some extent.

Marxism-Leninism-Maoism serves both to confirm and to complement certain views of the world that any Chinese leader would be likely to have. Its historical determinism strengthens confidence in China's destiny of greatness. Thus, Chinese leaders see China not only as big and potentially powerful, but also as righteous. They believe their views coincide with those of the great majority of the world's people. Consequently, they are confident that, despite temporary weakness, China will in time achieve its destined position of influence in the world. They recognize that setbacks are inevitable but that they can be endured, for they are convinced that ultimate success is certain if the Chinese people hold firm to their principles.

The strategic view expressed by China's leaders, in its purist, ideological form, can be summarized in the following propositions.

• Imperialism will never change its aggressive nature; therefore there can be no peace in the world until imperialism is destroyed.

• Imperialist regimes will be overthrown by the armed power of the people subject to such regimes.

• The United States is the leading imperialist power in the world today.

• The Soviet Union is now a social-imperialist power because revisionist leaders there have restored capitalism.

• The two superpowers are engaged in a worldwide struggle for supremacy. At times they compromise or even collaborate with each other to gain tactical advantages; they may temporarily concede spheres of interest to each other. But they are primarily rivals, because each seeks to dominate the world.

• The pretensions of the superpowers are meeting with growing resistance, in the form of both opposition from the peoples of those countries to their own governments and opposition from the other nations that they are attempting to dominate.

• China is the leading nation supporting the cause of revolution in the world and is therefore a prime object of the hostility of imperialist and social-imperialist leaders.

• The superpowers' struggle for supremacy may precipitate a world war, but there is a good chance that the growing strength of revolutionary forces will prevent it. As Mao has put it: "The danger of a new world war still exists, and the people of all countries must get prepared. But revolution is the main trend in the world today." He has also said: "With regard to the question of world war, there are but two possibilities: one is that the war will give rise to revolution and the other is that revolution will prevent war." [1]

The Tactical View

The stark and uncompromising strategic view outlined above does not determine day-to-day decisions or even medium-term policy goals

1. From an editorial in *People's Daily, Red Flag,* and *Liberation Army Daily,* Oct. 1, 1972; quoted in Foreign Broadcast Information Service, *Daily Report: People's Republic of China,* Oct. 2, 1972, p. B3.

in China's foreign policy. One reason for this is that the strategic view is a very long term one. Chinese leaders have sometimes spoken vaguely of the ultimate victory of world revolution as being fifty, one hundred, or even hundreds of years in the future. No goal that distant can determine relatively short-term objectives, especially when the ideology expressly allows for many zig-zags and apparent steps backward in the pursuit of that goal.

In making tactical foreign policy decisions, Chinese leaders seem to evaluate current power relationships quite realistically. They are strongly influenced by their consciousness of China's present weakness in military power and technological skill relative to its two principal adversaries. China's defensive strength protects it against conquest, even by the superpowers, but it is vulnerable to nuclear strikes or even to conventional attacks for limited objectives. Therefore, given the basic assumptions of the Chinese leaders about world politics, they must give high priority both to improving China's ability to defend itself and to reducing the risk of attack. This has resulted, on the one hand, in the diversion of substantial resources to producing nuclear weapons and other modern arms, and, on the other, to a variety of diplomatic and political moves aimed at keeping tension with the USSR at a tolerable level, improving relations with the United States, and seeking to forestall trends toward militarism in Japan. Thus, Peking's tactical posture toward these three big powers is basically defensive—a fact that tends to be obscured by the aggressive language used by Chinese propagandists.

The Chinese see the Soviet Union as the most serious potential threat to China today, not only militarily but also in a subversive sense as a rival for influence on communist parties throughout the world and on governments in the vicinity of China. It is as a military threat, however, that the USSR is the most worrisome to Chinese leaders. Since 1965, the Russians have built up powerful forces on China's border, which they continue to strengthen. They have taken a hostile attitude toward the Chinese leaders and even hinted that they were considering a preemptive strike on China's nuclear installations following the serious armed clashes on the Chinese-Soviet border in 1969. They invaded Czechoslovakia and proclaimed in the so-called Brezhnev doctrine their right to do the same with any aberrant "socialist" state. There is much evidence that the Chinese, for all these reasons, are seriously concerned about the Soviet military threat to China.

They are also concerned about the danger that Soviet "revisionism" poses to their political system. This concern reached an almost hysterical level during the Cultural Revolution. To some extent this resulted from the practice of pasting the label "revisionist" indiscriminately on all Mao's opponents in the Chinese Communist Party. Nevertheless, the evidence is convincing that at least since 1959 the Chinese have been much more worried about actual or suspected Soviet meddling in their internal affairs than they have been about U.S. meddling.[2]

Furthermore, the Soviets and the Chinese are now bitter rivals within the family of communist parties. Although the rivalry is worldwide, it is particularly intense with respect to ruling parties in states on the borders of China or the Soviet Union, such as North Korea, North Vietnam, or Rumania, where considerations of ideology are overlaid with considerations of the big power's security and national interests. We have no means of judging how the Chinese evaluate opposition to the Soviet leadership within the USSR, but they probably doubt that this opposition would grow strong enough in the next few years to reduce substantially the hostility of Soviet leaders toward China. It certainly seems unlikely that they believe, as their propaganda claims, that the opposition will soon overthrow the present Soviet leaders.

For all these reasons the Chinese leaders regard the Soviet Union as the greatest potential threat to China today. Reliable observers visiting China during the past year confirm this view. Concern with the Soviet threat must have been the chief reason why the Chinese leaders made the difficult decision to seek improvement of relations with the United States, even though fighting continued in Indochina and the Taiwan issue remained unresolved. A change in leadership in China might result in some easing of the tension between China and the Soviet Union, but the problems between them are now so basic and difficult to resolve that no far-reaching rapprochement is likely in the next few years.

Although the Chinese once viewed the United States as posing the greatest potential threat, they now see the United States as a less imminent military threat to China than the Soviet Union. In 1965, when the United States began to bomb North Vietnam and rapidly build up its

2. Note the references to "illicit relations" with foreign countries among the charges made against Defense Minister Peng Te-huai, purged in 1959, and Defense Minister Lin Piao, who appears to have fled the country in September 1971 after an unsuccessful attempt to seize power from Mao and to have died in a plane crash in Outer Mongolia.

ground forces in South Vietnam, the Chinese were seriously worried about possible military conflict with the United States. At that time the Soviet buildup on China's northern border had barely begun. But since 1969, the United States has withdrawn its forces from Vietnam and reduced its military strength elsewhere in East Asia, so that for several years U.S. forces in the vicinity of China have declined while those of the Soviet Union have increased. In his report to the Tenth National Congress of the Chinese Communist Party in August 1973, Chou En-lai said that "U.S. imperialism . . . has openly admitted that it is increasingly on the decline." He declared that, while China had to be prepared to meet attack from any quarter, it must be prepared particularly against surprise attack "by Soviet revisionist social-imperialism."

The Chinese must have been impressed not only by the withdrawal of U.S. forces in the vicinity of China but also by the strength of the opposition to the Vietnam war in the United States, including opposition in the Congress. Thus, it probably appears to the Chinese that the "imperialist" administration in Washington, whatever it might like to do, is less free to use military force in East Asia than the Soviet Union is.

The Chinese make a clear distinction between lightly armed, non-nuclear Japan and the superpowers, although they have been impressed by the rapid growth of the Japanese economy and the expansion of Japanese economic influence throughout East Asia. Following the Nixon-Sato communiqué of November 1969, in which Premier Sato declared Japan's interest in the security of South Korea and the Taiwan area, the Chinese seemed concerned that the United States was encouraging Japan to expand its military forces in order to take over a share of U.S. security responsibilities in Northeast Asia. Peking launched a vigorous propaganda campaign against Sato, alleging that "militarism" had revived in Japan. In August 1971, Chou En-lai said that an economy as highly developed as that of Japan "was bound to demand outward expansion" and that "economic expansion is bound to bring about military expansion." He charged that the United States was promoting militarism in Japan.[3] With the approach of President Nixon's visit to China, however, Chinese attacks on the "revival of Japanese militarism" fell off sharply. Apparently the prospect of better relations with the United States reduced anxiety about possible U.S.–Japanese collaboration in regional military activities that would be adverse to Chinese interests. Peking's leaders may also have wished to sweeten the atmosphere for

3. Interview with James Reston, *New York Times*, Aug. 10, 1971.

normalizing relations with Japan, which was achieved in September 1972. In any case, the Chinese have adopted a tolerant and even favorable view of the U.S.–Japanese security treaty and Japan's modest military establishment and have begun to cultivate better relations with both countries as a counter to Soviet pressures.

To sum up Peking's tactical view of the military threat to China over the next few years, the Chinese see a possible Soviet attack as the principal danger against which they must continue to allocate substantial resources for military preparations. Since 1973, however, they have referred to this threat in less alarmist terms than they used earlier, and they have reduced somewhat the proportion of resources allocated to defense. It seems probable that the increased deployment of medium- and intermediate-range ballistic missiles (MRBMs and IRBMs) has given Chinese leaders greater confidence that the USSR will be deterred from mounting a large-scale attack.

As for the United States, the Chinese probably expect that the trend of public opinion in this country in the wake of the unhappy Vietnam experience, together with Chinese success both in devoloping a nuclear deterrent and in cultivating better relations with the United States, will provide some assurance against any renewed U.S. military threat in the near future. This point of view would lead the Chinese to direct their armed forces and weapons program primarily at coping with the more imminent Soviet threat.

Japan probably is still seen as a potential threat over the long term: in Chou En-lai's words, that danger is "only budding."[4] Japanese military forces pose no significant threat to China today and thus need not be taken into account in designing Chinese forces. Moreover, the Chinese have indicated to the Japanese that they accept the present need for Japanese armed forces and even for the U.S.–Japan security treaty in the light of Soviet expansionist ambitions. The Chinese doubtless continue to be concerned over the possible increase of promilitary sentiment in Japan, but they probably see a reasonable chance that such a trend could be checked by the pressure of Japanese domestic opposition and by Chinese policies aimed at strengthening pro-Chinese, neutralist sentiment in Japan.

Although compelled by circumstances to adopt a defensive military stance toward other big powers, the Chinese leaders feel less constrained

4. Ibid.

politically. Here, China's size and the confidence that Chinese leaders have in China's destiny and the righteousness of their cause give Peking greater political influence than its limited military and economic power might suggest. Mao and his colleagues have always placed great emphasis on political and psychological factors, both domestically and internationally, relying on the view that "man is more important than weapons." On the international scene they perceive numerous contradictions—among the big powers, between the leaders and the people of the big powers, between the big powers and the lesser powers, and between the leaders and the people in many of the lesser powers. They seek to take advantage of these tensions by a variety of means, ranging from diplomatic moves through people-to-people activities to support for communist insurgents. Thus, they can be on the offensive politically while on the defensive militarily, so long as their actions run only a low risk of provoking a military reaction from one of the big powers.

This balance characterizes Chinese competition with the other big powers for influence in Asia and the rest of the world. Although this implies an adversary relationship with each of the other three powers, it is not a totally hostile relationship at all times. On the contrary, the Chinese rely increasingly on a strategy of maneuver in their relations with the USSR, the United States, and Japan that at times calls for improving relations with one of the three to pursue short-term ends vis-à-vis one or both of the others, as in the current effort to improve relations with the United States and Japan.

For the past several years China's foreign policy has been dominated by an obsessive suspicion of the Soviet Union and a consequent desire for rapprochement with the United States and Japan. Peking has agreed to set aside, at least temporarily, the Taiwan issue, which in the past had prevented improvement in U.S.–Chinese relations, and has switched from denunciation of NATO and the U.S.–Japan security treaty to an almost benign view of these alliances as checks on Soviet ambitions. Despite the importance to China of rapprochement with the United States and Japan, however, many points of potential friction remain, placing limits on how far rapprochement can go. The view that Chinese leaders take of the world, the advantages to China of retaining considerable freedom of maneuver with respect to all three of the other big powers, and the clashes of national interest China has with all three make full-scale alliance and close cooperation between China and any of the others improbable.

Military Force in Chinese Foreign Policy

An assessment of the role of military force as an instrument of Chinese foreign policy must ask the following questions. To what extent and in what ways have the Chinese relied on military force in the pursuit of foreign policy goals? Will China's growing nuclear capability make Peking likely to take greater risks than in the past in using military force on foreign soil? How do the Chinese perceive the military threat from the two superpowers and what options do they have in seeking to counter these threats?

Except when they believed China's territorial integrity to have been encroached upon or threatened, the Chinese have not used military force beyond their borders to attain foreign policy goals. They risked a major clash with a superpower only once, in Korea, and that only when they thought their own border gravely threatened. In the offshore islands crisis of 1958 and the Ussuri River clash of 1969, the Chinese pulled back quickly when the risk of war became too great. At the Indian border in 1962, having punished the Indians—whom the Chinese saw as having encroached on their territory—they promptly withdrew. They sent military units into North Vietnam to help the North Vietnamese counter air attacks and they also attacked the occasional U.S. plane that overflew the Chinese border, but they took care to avoid a large-scale clash with the United States. The Chinese have also forgone opportunities to mobilize their forces on the border to intimidate a weak neighbor, even though a state like Burma, which has no powerful foreign protector, might be vulnerable to such intimidation.

Maoist doctrine does not call for the participation of Chinese military forces in national liberation wars in other countries; on the contrary, it calls for maximum self-reliance on the part of indigenous forces. The Chinese have given political support, military equipment, and other kinds of material support to communist forces in other countries, but— except for North Korea and North Vietnam, both of which were in direct conflict with U.S. forces the amounts of military equipment furnished have been very small.

Not only is Chinese military doctrine predominantly defense oriented, but the Chinese have not produced significant amounts of the types of military equipment—especially naval and air equipment— that would be needed to project their military power any great distance beyond their borders. Neither have their troops been trained for such operations. Since the Cultural Revolution, the Chinese have placed even greater emphasis than before on organizing the nation's economy and its military forces to defend against invasion and air attack.

There is no evidence that the nuclear weapons thus far produced by China have significantly improved the nation's ability to gain foreign policy objectives by the direct use or threat of military force. On the contrary, the possession of a small and vulnerable nuclear force may have made the Chinese even more anxious to avoid the risk of conflict with one of the superpowers. They have shown sensitivity to veiled Soviet threats to carry out a preemptive attack on their nuclear facilities. In fact, instead of threatening others with nuclear weapons, the Chinese have put great emphasis on their pledge never to be the first to use them.

There is little reason to suppose that by the end of the 1970s China will be in a better position to risk a large-scale clash of arms with one of the superpowers. Given the long lead that the USSR and the United States have in conventional weapons and the expected modest rate of growth of Chinese industry, the gap between China and the superpowers in conventional weapons will probably remain large. China's nuclear force, which consists of approximately fifty MRBMs, some twenty to thirty IRBMs, and about one hundred TU-16 medium bombers,[5] would be tiny compared to the nuclear forces of the superpowers and would not have a completely credible second-strike capability. The massive difference in nuclear capabilities and the severity of losses to China if it took aggressive military action that provoked a nuclear exchange with the Soviet Union or the United States suggest that the Chinese will continue to be very cautious about using their forces outside their borders. In fact, the possession of a small nuclear force, most of which will continue to be vulnerable to a first strike, might well make the Chinese even more cautious in confronting the superpowers because of the increased risk that the adversary would strike first with nuclear weapons.

Even so small a Chinese nuclear force, however, would probably also make the USSR and the United States more cautious than in the past about a military clash with China. While China would theoretically be vulnerable to a first strike, the uncertainty of whether all its nuclear weapons could actually be wiped out in a first strike would force Soviet

---

5. See the Appendix for a more detailed estimate of the Chinese nuclear force.

and, eventually, American leaders, too, to consider their own possible losses if their calculation should be wrong. The Soviet Union and the United States are in somewhat different positions in this respect, however, for China can threaten Soviet territory today with nuclear weapons, while it is unlikely to have an intercontinental ballistic missile (ICBM) capable of reaching U.S. territory until the late 1970s at the earliest. Until then, Chinese nuclear weapons could be a possible threat only to the United States' allies in East Asia.

Since China cannot expect to have a military force in the 1970s strong enough to take large-scale offensive action against the Soviet Union or the United States, or against any state clearly under the protection of one of these powers, the Chinese probably will continue to equip their forces and develop strategies almost exclusively so as to maximize the defense of mainland China. This does not exclude planning for limited offensive thrusts if Soviet behavior at certain border points became intolerable to the Chinese, or if the Chinese saw their borders threatened with a large-scale invasion, as they apparently did in 1950 in Korea.

Countering the Soviet and U.S. Military Threats

In their military planning, the Chinese must consider three possible forms of Soviet attack on China.

Nuclear attack. The Soviet Union could wipe out most of China's modern industry and the people who operate it in a nuclear attack. The Chinese have no way of preventing such an attack. They can only rely on the considerable inhibitions against the use of nuclear weapons by anyone (including particularly the impact on the U.S. and its allies that the use of nuclear weapons by the USSR against China would have) and on the deterrent value of such strategic nuclear weapons as China itself can produce in the coming years.

Massive conventional attack. With their superior conventional forces, the Soviets could probably invade China and occupy some of the principal cities and main transportation lines, on the pattern of the Japanese invasion, but with the additional advantage of having a nuclear backstop. Such an attack could be supported by selective strategic or tactical nuclear strikes.

Limited attack for a special purpose. Such attacks might include, for example, a conventional "surgical" strike or overland assault to take out China's nuclear facilities, fomenting and then supporting a minority rebellion in Sinkiang, or nipping off the economically important and exposed salient, Manchuria, as the Japanese did in 1931.

Given the Soviet military buildup on the Chinese border since 1965, a nuclear or limited attack could be carried out with little or no warning, but preparations to invade and occupy a large part of China would presumably take some time.

Chinese military planners probably regard the U.S. capability to carry out a full-scale nuclear attack on China's cities or a conventional surgical strike on China's nuclear facilities as at least equal to that of the USSR. The United States is obviously in a less favorable position, however, to attempt a large-scale invasion and occupation of China or to try to seize Manchuria. Securing and maintaining beachheads for the invasion of China would be far more costly and difficult than invading China overland from the Soviet border. Even if it could be established, a beachhead would be a particularly attractive target for a nuclear weapon, and the United States could not count on wiping out all China's nuclear weapons in preemptive strikes before landing on the mainland. China's other land borders are protected from U.S. land assault either by the buffer states of North Korea and North Vietnam or by the extremely rugged and difficult terrain along the rest of China's southern border. Preparations for a large-scale U.S. invasion of China would thus have to be massive, thereby providing early warning.

Since the Chinese see the Soviet Union as more of a threat in the near future than the United States, their defensive military preparations, although probably designed insofar as possible to be usable against either superpower (this is particularly true for long-lead-time items, such as strategic nuclear weapons), will tend to be weighted in favor of those likely to be most useful against Soviet actions.

The magnitude and variety of possible military threats to China by the Soviet Union or the United States pose a difficult problem for Chinese strategic planners. Resources are scarce and the requirements for weapons and forces to counter all possible threats are very large. Moreover, resources diverted today to immediate military uses are not available for building the broad industrial base that would both contribute to economic development in general and put China in a better position ten years from now to compete with the other big powers in producing advanced weapons systems. The Chinese leaders thus face difficult choices in striking the optimum balance between today's military requirements and the future economic development of the nation. Further choices must be made about the allocation of resources among the various possible military strategies and the weapons systems needed to support these strategies.

Chinese leaders have in the past differed significantly as to the best military strategy for the defense of China and the allocation of resources in support of that strategy. There is every reason to assume that such debates will continue. Of course, advocates of a particular strategy, in China as elsewhere, are influenced by their own special interests. Political leaders tend to espouse military strategies helpful to their domestic political purposes, and military leaders tend to favor strategies that give their service or military region a larger claim on the resources of the state than other strategies would. Yet all must defend their choice of strategy in terms of the external threat. The available evidence suggests that the debate is likely to focus on choosing among the following three broad strategic options.

• *The rapid expansion of strategic nuclear weapons, relatively few resources devoted to expensive conventional weapons, and heavy reliance on a "people's war" of attrition as protection against invasion* (the Maoist strategy). The rationale for this strategy is that it is the nuclear threat that is the most dangerous to China, and it can be deterred only by nuclear weapons; therefore, available resources should be concentrated on producing such weapons as quickly as possible. To attempt to compete seriously with the USSR or the United States in conventional weapons would divert too many resources from nuclear weapons and from the building of a strong, decentralized economy that would both provide the best base from which to fight a defensive people's war and offer poor targets to nuclear weapons.

The main weakness of this strategy is that it would not provide adequate protection against a Soviet effort to seize a piece of China. The Chinese would be short of the conventional forces necessary to put up a strong defense of Sinkiang or Manchuria and make its conquest costly to the USSR. They would have to rely on the chance that their growing nuclear force would not only serve as an increasing deterrent to a Soviet nuclear attack but would also reduce the risk of a large-scale conventional attack by creating the fear that the Chinese might in desperation try to wound the USSR by attacking important centers with nuclear weapons, even though they knew the Soviets could respond with a devastating nuclear attack on China.

This strategy would also leave the Chinese relatively ill prepared to meet a U.S. attack launched from adjacent nations or directed against the China coast. It might appear to the Chinese, however, that this risk was worth taking, given current trends in U.S. policy. If such an attack were judged improbable over the next few years, the time gained might be best used to improve China's ability to deter the greater long-term threat—the nuclear threat.

• *Continuing development of strategic nuclear weapons at a moderate pace, while committing more resources to modernizing conventional forces and putting less emphasis on people's war* (the military professionals' strategy). The rationale for this strategy is that the most likely Soviet attack on China would be a limited one aimed at destroying China's nuclear facilities or seizing a piece of Chinese territory. China already has enough nuclear weapons to offer some deterrence to a Soviet nuclear attack and, even if the current rate of production is not stepped up, this force will steadily increase. These weapons, together with political inhibitions on the use of nuclear weapons by the USSR, make a Soviet nuclear attack unlikely. A forced draft effort to speed up production of strategic nuclear weapons at the cost of delaying the modernization of conventional forces would not significantly improve the odds against Soviet nuclear attack. An all-out conventional attack by the USSR against China is also unlikely because of China's great defensive power against a long-term war of attrition.

Therefore, China should concentrate on preparing itself better against the most likely contingency by putting large amounts of resources into modernizing its conventional armed forces. Most emphasis should be placed on ground and air forces, since the Soviet naval threat is less dangerous and could be met by investment in such relatively inexpensive items as motor torpedo boats. Naval power, especially submarines, would be much more important against a U.S. attack, but since the Soviet threat is more imminent, these naval requirements could safely be given a lower priority.

• *Balanced development of strategic nuclear weapons, modernized conventional forces, and preparations for people's war* (the bureaucratic strategy). The rationale for this strategy is to strike a compromise among conflicting judgments as to the urgency of the various threats and thus to balance the claims on resources of the various armed services and departments of government. It would also balance the claims of the military professionals who are central-government oriented, such as those who run the strategic nuclear program, and the claims of powerful commanders in the military regions, whose political power tends to be strengthened by the economic decentralization called for by the people's war concept and whose desires for military modernization are more likely to focus on the requirements of the army than of the air force and navy. To some extent it would represent a compromise in the continuing debate between "reds" and "experts" in the Chinese Communist system.

Current trends in China suggest that the bureaucrats and the military professionals are probably in the ascendancy over the Maoists, but which group may ultimately win out is less important for the purposes of this analysis than that all three groups have a strongly defensive orientation. It is the overwhelming concern with the need to defend China against a hostile outside world that stands out in all Chinese military planning.

The Use of Force in Southeast Asia

Even though China will remain much weaker militarily than the two superpowers through the 1970s, it will continue to tower over its smaller neighbors to the south. Will the Chinese be tempted to use military force there when the United States withdraws all its forces from mainland Southeast Asia, relying on their growing nuclear force to deter the United States from intervening again? Given the past prudence of the Chinese in using military force beyond their borders and their present preoccupation with improving China's ability to deter or resist military attack by a superpower, it is hard to imagine the Chinese launching their forces into Southeast Asia in the next few years. True, their growing nuclear force and the U.S. withdrawal from mainland Southeast Asia might afford them marginally greater assurance that the United States would not intervene militarily, but it seems doubtful that the gains would be worth the risks and costs that would be incurred.

In the first place, a military conflict in Southeast Asia, even on a small scale, would divert resources badly needed for both defensive preparations against possible Soviet attack and economic development. Even if such a war ended quickly, to the extent that the Chinese desired to maintain control over the defeated nation—and this would presumably be the objective of any invasion—they would be assuming an open-ended responsibility for supporting occupation forces or continuing to supply the local government with military and economic aid, or both.

Moreover, aggression by China against a Southeast Asian state, even though it did not result in military confrontation with the United States, would necessarily put a stop to the efforts of the Chinese leaders to improve relations with the United States, which they have desired in order to strengthen China's position relative to the USSR—an objective that would seem to outweigh any possible gains from invasion of a Southeast Asian state. Chinese military action would also alarm other Southeast Asian states and might reverse the trend toward the withdrawal of the U.S. military presence in the area. Much stronger ties between the United States and Indonesia, for example, would be a likely consequence.

Resort by China to overt military aggression in Southeast Asia would cause the Soviet Union, the United States, and Japan to revise their reading of Chinese intentions. The probable result would be for all to devote more resources to military preparations against possible Chinese threats. This would tend to create the very danger of encirclement by hostile forces that has worried the Chinese in the past.

Still another cost to China of military aggression in Southeast Asia would be severe damage to the image the Chinese have cultivated in the Third World. Chinese denunciations of the Soviet invasion of Czechoslovakia would lose much of their force, for instance, and in such circumstances Chinese protestations that China would never be a superpower would have a hollow ring.

Finally, it is difficult to see why the Chinese would feel any strong compulsion to take an action likely to be so damaging to the achievement of other objectives. The withdrawal of U.S. forces would remove any fear the Chinese might have had that their own frontier was threatened from Southeast Asia. China's entry into the United Nations and increasing participation in world politics would seem to improve its prospects for increasing its influence and pursuing its interests in Southeast Asia by political and economic means, and therefore would diminish any need to resort to more drastic measures. Moreover, unless there is some radical modification of the Chinese leaders' view of the world, they will probably be prepared to wait for local revolutionary forces to make themselves felt in due course in Southeast Asia—willing to nourish them by moral and material aid to communist insurgents perhaps, but seeing no need to become militarily involved.

Political Uses of China's Nuclear Weapons

In addition to imposing upon the Soviet Union and the United States the need for greater caution in risking military conflict with China, the acquisition of nuclear weapons has enhanced China's prestige and influence in the world. China will probably learn—as Britain and France have—that relatively small nuclear forces do not greatly increase a nation's influence in the long run, but for the time being they have added to China's clout. Political analysts all over the world now focus on the interaction of the "big three." But perhaps most important, the leaders of noncommunist nations near China have begun to consider whether China's possession of nuclear weapons will affect the willingness of the United States to carry out its defense commitments in that region, a willingness already called into question in the eyes of many Southeast Asians by the impact of the Vietnam war on the American people.

China can also now claim a special voice in arms control matters by virtue of being a nuclear power. It can either display its importance by joining in arms control negotiations or agreements with other nuclear powers or it can pose as the champion of the nonnuclear powers against the superpowers—the role it has chosen so far. Either tactic draws attention to China's possession of nuclear weapons and thus serves to enhance China's prestige.

There are limitations, however, on China's ability to use its possession of nuclear weapons to increase its political influence. For one thing, once a nation has crossed the nuclear threshold and reaped whatever gains it can from that act, adding to the size of its nuclear force—short of approaching parity with the United States or the USSR—does not produce commensurate increments of political influence. The one exception to this rule might be China's acquisition of long-range ICBMs, which conceivably could increase substantially the impact of Peking's nuclear posture on U.S.–Japanese relations, for once U.S. cities came within range of Chinese nuclear weapons, some Japanese might question whether the United States would risk San Francisco to protect Tokyo.

The Chinese will probably find, however, that it is difficult to use their nuclear capability in any direct fashion to achieve political objectives. They would pay a high price, for example, were they to attempt "nuclear blackmail," as some observers have feared they might. In the first place, they would run the risk that the intended victim might not yield to the threat to use nuclear weapons against it if it did not concede whatever China was demanding. The Chinese would then either have to use military force to carry out their threat—incurring all the costs described above—or permit their bluff to be called. Such a failure in the game of nuclear blackmail would cause triple damage to China. Of course there would be a loss of prestige. But more important, China's attempt to use nuclear weapons to coerce its neighbors would validate the views of those in the Soviet Union and the United States who hold that the Chinese respond only to force and must be dealt with from a position of overwhelming military strength. In addition, Peking's efforts to achieve a position of moral leadership in the Third World would suffer a serious setback.

Even if the nuclear blackmail succeeded and the neighboring state was coerced into accepting Chinese demands, the cost of success would also be high. Whatever gains the Chinese made by inspiring greater fear in other nations would probably be more than counterbalanced, first by the adverse reactions of the superpowers and Third World nations to this demonstration of Chinese power and belligerence, and second by the probability that Japan as well as India would decide to follow the Chinese example and acquire nuclear weapons, both to be able to defend themselves against Chinese nuclear blackmail and to increase their own power and influence in the world. For all these reasons, it is unlikely that the Chinese will attempt nuclear blackmail, forsaking their strongly and consistently stated position that they will never be first to use nuclear weapons.

There is a further reason why the Chinese are unlikely in the next few years to use their nuclear weapons in a blustering way: they will be strongly motivated by the need to gain time. They probably expect that with the passage of years they will be able to reduce gradually the military and technological gap between China and the superpowers. They particularly need time to build a credible second-strike nuclear deterrent, without which they must continue to feel vulnerable to a preemptive first strike. Moreover, Chinese leaders hold that revolutionary forces will gain momentum in the world with the passage of time. Taking the long view and being confident that history works in their favor, they probably will continue to believe that it is neither necessary nor wise to risk high political costs by attempting to use nuclear weapons to attain short-term objectives in Asia.

Thus, the only political advantages the Chinese are likely to gain from their possession of nuclear weapons are the generalized respect and attention accruing to any state that is a nuclear power. How much influence nuclear status will add to that which a nonnuclear China would already possess is uncertain. It may well be a declining asset, as suggested above, if, as time passes, neighboring states learn that Chinese nuclear blackmail is a less fearsome specter than they first thought.

Chinese Policies toward Japan and Korea

The three fundamental objectives of Chinese policy toward Japan are: first, to strengthen pro-Chinese sentiment in Japan and draw Japan closer to China, and away from the Soviet Union; second, to prevent Japan from building a powerful military force with nuclear weapons; and, third, to limit the expansion of Japanese influence in Asia, especially in South Korea, Taiwan, and Southeast Asia.

There are inherent contradictions in the pursuit of these policies. Efforts to draw Japan into a closer relationship with China tend to conflict with efforts to limit the expansion of Japanese influence in Asia. Moreover, if rivalry came increasingly to dominate the relationship between China and Japan, Chinese possession of nuclear weapons would tend to strengthen the position of those Japanese—now a small minority—who believe Japan should have nuclear weapons also.

The very existence of China's nuclear force, even without any attempt by the Chinese to brandish it at Japan, affects Japanese attitudes toward China in various ways. On the one hand, it probably strengthens those pacifistic, proneutralist, antimilitary groups who argue that it is vital for Japan to cultivate the friendship of China in order to avoid another war. On the other hand, every time the Chinese test a nuclear weapon they provoke an adverse reaction from the Japanese government and the bulk of the Japanese people. Moreover, China's possession of nuclear weapons makes it more likely that Japan will cling to the security treaty with the United States or rearm massively, or both.

The Chinese so far have played down their possession of nuclear weapons. They have called for the total abolition and destruction of such weapons, have declared that they would never be the first to use them, and in general have avoided military threats or rocket-rattling. Among their reasons for taking this posture is undoubtedly the desire to minimize the adverse effect of their nuclear status on their relation with Japan. They would like, if possible, to enlist Japanese support in putting pressure on the superpowers to limit their nuclear forces or inhibit their use. Were the Chinese to throw their military weight around, emphasizing their possession of a nuclear force, the effect on Japan would almost certainly be counterproductive. Rather than intimidating the Japanese, it would be more likely to arouse their nationalistic spirit and convince them that Japan, too, must have nuclear weapons. Thus, China's desire for a nonnuclear Japan constitutes one of the most important inhibitions against China's seeking diplomatic gains by calling attention to its nuclear power.

This confronts the Chinese with a problem as they consider whether or when to proceed with the testing and deployment of ICBMs. On the one hand, deploying a long-range ICBM would have the desirable effect of bringing American cities within range of China's nuclear weapons, thus creating a strategic deterrent that would be useful in the event of any future U.S.–Chinese military confrontation. On the other hand, the existence of such a deterrent might cause the Japanese to question the credibility of the U.S. nuclear deterrent, as did, for example, General Gallois in the debate over the French nuclear force. This could weaken or even lead to the dissolution of the U.S.–Japan security treaty and might in time cause the Japanese to follow the French example and proceed to build their own nuclear force. Thus, uncertainty about the effect on Japan, along with the priority given defenses against the USSR and the decline of the immediate U.S. military threat, could be a factor causing the Chinese to delay the production of a long-range ICBM.

Chinese policies toward Japan are particularly concerned with Korea, a traditional arena of conflict for China and Japan. Chinese suspicions of Japanese intentions toward Korea increased after the Nixon-Sato communiqué of November 1969, in which Premier Sato characterized the security of South Korea as "essential" to the security of Japan. Since the U.S. commitment to the defense of South Korea serves as a buffer that prevents any direct confrontation between China and Japan, the Chinese are probably somewhat ambivalent toward the presence of U.S. forces in South Korea, and might in time be receptive to the idea of international arrangements that would stabilize the situation in Korea, prevent a Chinese-Japanese confrontation over Korea, and in general permit them to downplay their possession of nuclear weapons in their policies toward Japan.

Chinese Policy toward India

The Chinese have shown relatively little concern about Indian military power. China proper has never been invaded by India, as it was by Japan, and the mountain barrier between the two nations presents an almost insurmountable obstacle to any large-scale invasion attempt. Moreover, the stinging defeat handed the Indians in 1962 has given the Chinese confidence that they can handle the Indians militarily. This view is strengthened by internal weaknesses in India that the Chinese see as providing favorable ground for the development of revolutionary forces. The principal concern of the Chinese is that the Indians might, through the Dalai Lama, stir up trouble for them among the Tibetans.

The demonstrated ability of the Chinese to defend their borders against Indian encroachment with conventional forces means that they have not needed to depend on nuclear weapons to deter or defend against an Indian conventional attack. Neither have the Chinese found it necessary to brandish their nuclear weapons or to attempt nuclear blackmail against the Indians. Nevertheless, from the Indian viewpoint, China's nuclear weapons give Peking a military advantage over India, and this has exerted strong pressure on India to acquire nuclear weapons of its own, rather than to have to rely on the protection of a superpower that might prove fickle. This is a principal reason why India refused to sign the nuclear nonproliferation treaty and proceeded with the underground explosion of a nuclear device in May 1974.

Although the Indians have announced that their nuclear detonation was aimed at developing nuclear explosives for peaceful use rather than for weapons, the explosion probably will compel the Chinese to rethink their nuclear strategy, for they cannot be sure that the Indians are not secretly producing some form of nuclear weapon. The growing closeness of India to the USSR since the two nations cooperated in helping to establish Bangla Desh has caused India to appear increasingly to Peking as an element in a Soviet scheme to contain China. The Indian nuclear explosion is likely to increase these Chinese suspicions.

The emergence of a potential nuclear threat from India considerably complicates China's defense problem. The Chinese will have to consider whether to target some of their small number of nuclear weapons on India to act as a deterrent to Indian use of nuclear weapons. They will also have to decide how to respond to the probable pressures from Pakistan for added Chinese help to counter a possible Indian attack, perhaps including nuclear defense guarantees or even a Pakistani request for assistance in producing their own nuclear weapons. In addition, they will have to sort out the implications of a nuclear India for their policies toward both India and the USSR. They might decide, for example, that the time has come for Chinese initiatives to improve relations with India in an effort to diminish Soviet influence over that country.

Peking might also wish to reconsider its stand on the proliferation of nuclear weapons in the light of the Indian nuclear explosion. It could depart from its past policy of not assisting other countries to produce weapons and give technical aid to Pakistan. But given the uncertainty as to whether the Indians are, in fact, producing nuclear weapons and the impetus that Chinese nuclear assistance to Pakistan might give to proliferation generally, the Chinese will probably be reluctant to take this step. They will be particularly interested in whether Japanese re-action to the Indian detonation weakens the opposition to nuclear weap-ons in Japan. The Chinese would presumably wish to react to the Indian move in ways that would help to sustain the Japanese opposition to nuclear weapons and might, therefore, take a less critical attitude to-ward the nonproliferation treaty than they have in the past, or even tacitly support it.

India's nuclear explosion will probably make China even less likely than in the past to utter nuclear threats against India or to take pro-vocative actions on the frontier. This estimate of probable Chinese behavior toward India reinforces the conclusions already drawn that Peking would gain little and might lose much from abandoning its low-key, no-first-use nuclear posture in order to use nuclear weapons to try to intimidate other nations.

Conclusions

The possession of nuclear weapons probably will not, in the 1970s, alter China's propensity toward caution in the use of its military forces beyond its borders, for Chinese leaders, despite their advocacy of world revolution, take a realistic view of power relationships. The disparity between the strength of China's armed forces and those of the super-powers, both conventional and nuclear, will remain great. It is difficult to produce persuasive reasons why China might either threaten one of its weaker neighbors with nuclear weapons or launch a large-scale attack on it with conventional forces, even a nation that was not protected by a credible U.S. commitment. The long-term cost of such aggressive be-havior by China would be high and the gains uncertain, for it would not only stimulate the superpowers to devote more resources to military strength, but also would probably cause Japan as well as India to go nuclear. Thus, the main advantages to China of the nuclear weapons it will have in the seventies will be (1) to make the Soviet Union and the United States more cautious in risking a military clash with China, and (2) to secure whatever general increase in prestige and influence attaches to being a nuclear power.

CHAPTER TWO

China's Nuclear Weapons and U.S. Defense

The development of China's nuclear capabilities has already influenced U.S. defense policy and will have a growing importance and impact throughout the 1970s and beyond. Although China's detonation of a nuclear device in 1964 was an important event, its recent acquisition of nuclear delivery systems has implications of far greater consequence. China already has a usable force of medium-range jet bombers and has begun to deploy medium- and intermediate-range ballistic missiles (MRBMs and IRBMs). It is expected by the late 1970s to have completed the deployment of a modest force based on these systems that will be capable of covering most targets in Asia and the USSR.

The increase in China's regional nuclear capacity clearly affects U.S. interests and commitments in Asia. Of even greater significance to the United States, however, is the prospect that China might deploy a small force of intercontinental ballistic missiles (ICBMs) by the 1980s. Chinese capability to reach targets in the United States with nuclear weapons would not only introduce a new and complicating element into U.S. security policies toward Asia, but would also raise new kinds of issues relating to nuclear deterrence, the stability of the worldwide strategic balance, and future military-strategic relations between the United States and the USSR.

How might the Chinese nuclear force affect U.S. deterrence capabilities and defense policies in Asia? And how should the United States define its regional and strategic defense postures so as to minimize the problems and possible risks posed by a growing Chinese nuclear force yet maintain the objectives of making progress toward arms control and improving relations with China?

28

Strategic Doctrine

The emerging Chinese nuclear force raises the question of whether the United States should rely primarily on deterrence with respect to China or seek an alternative strategy. The United States has relied on deterrence in its policy toward the Soviet Union, in part because it recognized that no feasible combination of offensive and defensive measures could provide a reliable "damage denial" capability,[1] or even a meaningful "damage limiting" capability,[2] against Soviet strategic forces. In relation to China, however, the overwhelming superiority of U.S. strategic nuclear power has led some analysts to consider the feasibility and desirability of seeking a damage denial capability against Peking, by a combination of defensive and offensive means.

The Case against Attempting Damage Denial

Existing and planned U.S. offensive forces, at least through the end of the 1970s, could destroy a substantial fraction of the Chinese nuclear force in a counterforce strike, since China's forces will remain small and vulnerable. The United States could add to this counterforce capability by improving the accuracy of its offensive missiles or by procuring new strategic missiles and aircraft systems at a more rapid pace than presently planned. There could be no certainty, however, in the unlikely event that U.S. leaders considered a preemptive strike with these improved offensive forces, that it would be totally successful. Given the difficulty of mounting a coordinated strike, the Chinese might be able to launch some of their nuclear missiles "on warning,"[3] and even if not, a few of their weapons could be expected to escape destruction. To give a theoretical example, calculation of the probable results of a strike by one MIRVed Poseidon missile[4] carrying ten warheads against each of one hundred "soft" Chinese missile sites indicates that, while

1. *Damage denial capability* is the ability to prevent damage to one's own country by destroying, either before or after launch, all the enemy's nuclear weapons capable of striking one's own country.

2. *Damage limiting capability* is the ability to destroy enough of the enemy's weapons to reduce significantly damage to one's own country.

3. That is, launch their missiles on learning that a U.S. attack had been launched, but before it struck its target.

4. An advanced submarine-launched missile carrying multiple independently targetable reentry vehicles (MIRVs).

there would be a 99 percent chance of destroying at least ninety-five sites, there would be only a 35 percent chance of destroying *all* the sites. Moreover, in the 1980s, as the Chinese nuclear force increases, as hardened or mobile missiles are introduced into China, and as improved Chinese warning and alert capabilities are deployed, the effectiveness of a strategy of damage denial by means of a counterforce strike will decrease.

It would theoretically be possible to supplement improved U.S. offensive forces with a nationwide antiballistic missile (ABM) system, along the lines of the Sentinel or full Safeguard programs.[5] However, the accords reached in the Strategic Arms Limitation Talks (SALT) between the United States and the USSR preclude this type of ABM deployment. But even if it were not precluded, such an ABM system would be inadvisable. While it could limit damage to the U.S. from a Chinese ICBM attack, it could not be relied upon to prevent damage; moreover, it could not protect our allies against attack by China's regional nuclear forces. At a minimum, one or two U.S. cities would probably suffer severe damage and Japan would face the possibility of catastrophic destruction. Furthermore, as the Chinese nuclear force grows in size and improves in quality, the effectiveness of a nationwide ABM system in the United States would steadily decline, however much the United States might try to improve its technical effectiveness.

In brief, even if the United States were to enlarge its offensive forces and construct a nationwide ABM system, it could not acquire a capability to deny Peking the option of inflicting severe damage on this nation or on America's allies or overseas bases.

The Case for Relying on Nuclear Deterrence

The basic objective of U.S. security policies vis-à-vis China, therefore, must be to deter China from considering the use of nuclear weapons against our allies, and, as ICBMs are added to Peking's weapons inventory, to deter China from considering nuclear attacks against the continental United States. In fact, the Chinese have already stated that they would never be the first to use nuclear weapons, and it is difficult to envisage situations in which they might consider launching a nuclear first strike. Nonetheless, the existence of Chinese nuclear forces and the

5. Descriptions of the Sentinel and Safeguard systems can be found in Abram Chayes and Jerome B. Wiesner (eds.), *ABM: An Evaluation of the Decision to Deploy an Antiballistic Missile System* (Signet, 1969).

potential for conflict between the two nations make it necessary for the United States to maintain an effective and credible deterrent.

There is no reason why the United States cannot and should not rely on a deterrence policy vis-à-vis China similar to its policy toward the Soviet Union.[6] Chinese leaders appreciate the destructive potential of nuclear weapons, and the positions they have taken on nuclear weapons indicate that they understand, at least in general terms, the principles of deterrence. They have to assume the virtual certainty of U.S. nuclear retaliation in the event of a Chinese nuclear attack upon the United States and accept a high risk of similar retaliation should China attack a U.S. ally. The combination of the high risk of U.S. retaliation and the enormous damage such retaliation would inflict on China can be relied upon to prevent Chinese leaders from deciding to launch nuclear weapons against the United States, or against U.S. overseas bases or allies. That the Chinese do not flaunt their nuclear weapons and assert repeatedly that they will never be the first to use them suggest that they are keenly aware of these considerations.

The United States maintains a minimum deterrent capability to kill at least 25 percent of the population of the Soviet Union and destroy or damage 50 percent of its industry. It is questionable whether the same criteria for "assured destruction" would apply to China. Because of the predominantly rural distribution of the Chinese population (only 8 percent of China's population is located in the largest 150 cities) the weapons requirements to inflict such levels of population damage would be extremely large. On the other hand, since leadership, large-scale industry, and nuclear production facilities tend to be concentrated in relatively few areas in China, a few hundred U.S. warheads are all that would be required to destroy most of China's industry and its major urban centers. Since China will lack the capabilities to undertake a preemptive strike on U.S. nuclear weapons systems, or to cause any significant attrition of U.S. systems during penetration, the United States need plan only a few hundred warheads against Chinese targets to create an effective deterrent. Thus, one can be reasonably confident that the potential damage to China that a few hundred nuclear warheads could inflict would ensure that Chinese leaders would refrain from considering the launching of any nuclear weapons.

6. This theme is developed at some length by A. Doak Barnett in "A Nuclear China and U.S. Arms Policy," *Foreign Affairs*, vol. 48 (April 1970), pp. 428–42.

U.S. Capability to Deter Both the USSR and China

The United States, with its existing forces, can maintain a capacity to deter China from considering nuclear attacks without detracting from its deterrent needs vis-à-vis the USSR. This is because the United States planned its strategic forces conservatively, and so possesses greater capabilities than are required to deter the USSR.[7] For example, by the late 1970s, the United States could have over 10,000 deployed nuclear warheads deliverable by missiles or bomber forces. If as many as 500 of these warheads were assigned to deter China, the capabilities vis-à-vis the Soviet Union would not be significantly weakened. Even in the unlikely event that the Soviet Union were to launch a first strike, the surviving U.S. nuclear force would be sufficient to retaliate against the USSR while still retaining an adequate deterrent against China. The recent limited SALT agreement, which "freezes" the number of U.S. ICBMs, will not alter this situation. Indeed, since this agreement will permit the United States to continue developing its MIRVs while limiting ABMs in the Soviet Union as well as the United States, a large number of warheads should be available for deterrence against China without weakening the U.S. capability to deter the USSR.[8] It will not be necessary, in short, to build additional forces to deal with China, since current U.S. strategic programs aimed at deterring the Soviet Union will provide sufficient weapons to deter China as well.

The Damage Limitation Option

While the United States cannot, as pointed out above, attain a damage denial capability against China, it will have an appreciable damage limitation capability even if it does not add to the improvements in its strategic offensive force now projected for the next five years. It would be possible to improve the damage limitation capability against China further by technical improvement in both offensive and defense weapons systems, but any extensive defensive system against Chinese missiles has been ruled out by the agreement between the United States and the USSR that each will limit itself to one ABM site with not over 100 missiles. This agreement is so fundamental to the effort to maintain a stable

7. For a comprehensive analysis of U.S. strategic arms capabilities, see Alton Quanbeck and Barry Blechman, *Strategic Forces: Issues for the Mid-Seventies* (Brookings Institution, 1973).
8. See Chapter 3 for a discussion of the SALT agreements and their implications.

strategic balance with the Soviet Union that it would make little sense to consider abandoning it for the sake of marginal gains in the U.S. damage limitation capacity against China.

Even if an extensive ABM system were not ruled out by the U.S.–Soviet agreement, it is doubtful that the marginal improvement it would make in the ability of the United States to limit damage would justify its great expense or outweigh its possible adverse effects on U.S. foreign policy. While an ABM system designed against China would afford some protection against accidentally launched missiles, would make it more difficult for China to acquire and maintain a credible nuclear deterrent, and might reduce pressure on an American president to launch a first strike in a crisis, it would in other respects be counterproductive.

Chinese leaders might well view it as threatening, since it would make more plausible the possibility of a U.S. offensive strike. Rather than decreasing Peking's propensity to stress nuclear weapons, such a U.S. policy might impel it to place increased emphasis on its nuclear programs and devote additional resources to them—for instance, in further development of regional forces targeted on U.S. allies, who would not be protected by American ABMs, or in accelerated development of penetration-aids to enhance the effectiveness of Chinese ICBMs. Thus, by heightening the Chinese sense of insecurity, a damage limitation policy could create new obstacles to the improvement of U.S. relations with China and progress in arms control.[9]

Moreover, by exacerbating Chinese fears of a U.S. attack, such a policy could increase the dangers of a Chinese missile launch in a crisis situation, thereby, paradoxically, diminishing U.S. security. Indeed, if the United States were to adopt such a policy, some American leaders might be inclined to argue that our damage limiting capability should make us willing to consider taking greater risks in policies toward China—and this, too, would be undesirable.

Nuclear Stability

It seems clear that any clash between the United States and China involving nuclear weapons is extremely unlikely. U.S. strategic plan-

9. See testimony by Alice Hsieh, in *ABM, MIRV, SALT, and the Nuclear Arms Race*, Hearings before the Senate Foreign Relations Committee, 91 Cong. 2 sess. (1970), pp. 133–41.

ning must consider, however, how to minimize the danger that such an
unlikely event might lead to strategic war between the United States
and the USSR.

Danger of Accidental War

The U.S.–Soviet agreements on the hot line, preventing nuclear war,
and reducing the risk of accidental launches should minimize the danger
that any Chinese missile launched against either the United States or the
USSR might inadvertently trigger an all-out U.S.–Soviet exchange.
However, if the United States were compelled to overfly the Soviet
Union with its land-based Minuteman ICBMs in retaliation against a
Chinese attack, there would be substantial risk of triggering a U.S.–
Soviet clash. Thus, for nuclear deterrence against China the U.S. should
rely primarily on its sea-based missiles, supplemented by strategic
bombers based in the Pacific or flying routes outside of the Soviet Union.
U.S. bombers probably would be capable of penetrating China's air
defense with little attrition, and thus would be capable of flying more
than one mission against the Chinese mainland.

The question also arises whether there would be risks of accidental
nuclear war arising out of a U.S.–Chinese confrontation, particularly as
the Chinese nuclear force grows. One can conceive of circumstances in
which such risks might arise. In a time of tension, for example, Chinese
missiles might be placed in a state of high alert, ready to be launched
"on warning," since the Chinese would recognize that their system
would not be able to withstand a heavy U.S. strike. Placing missiles on
high alert increases the risk of an accidental or unauthorized firing. How
dangerous such a situation would be, however, would depend in part
on the extent to which the Chinese had developed fully reliable command and control procedures. One can also speculate that if Chinese
leaders feared that a U.S. counterforce strike was imminent, there might
be those who would argue for launching some of their missiles early—
as a show of force, to avert the danger of preemption, or simply as a
panic reaction. This eventuality is admittedly unlikely, though not inconceivable. And under certain circumstances, concern that Chinese
missiles might be launched by accident, or the fear that Peking might
misread our intentions and launch its missiles first, might tempt some
U.S. leaders to consider a preemptive strike in order to limit damage to
this nation. This too seems most unlikely, but is a theoretical possibility.
All of these dangers could be reduced through various kinds of arms

control agreements or understandings, such as those discussed in Chapter 4.

The Chinese Nuclear Force and the U.S.–USSR Strategic Balance

The growth of China's nuclear force raises the issue of whether the strategic balance can remain stable in a "triangular" relationship in which the United States and the USSR are seeking to deter China as well as each other and China is seeking to acquire a deterrent against both superpowers. Unlike the French and British nuclear forces, which are directed against the Soviet Union but not against the United States, the Chinese nuclear force introduces a new element into the strategic equation, since China is a potential adversary of both superpowers.

In this situation, the Soviet Union seems to be willing, like the United States, to rely on deterrence against China. There have been no public Soviet statements favoring an "anti-China" ABM, for example, and Soviet negotiators apparently took the lead in advocating low-level ABM limitations in SALT. The USSR evidently believes it can satisfy its deterrent requirements for China without detracting from its strategic objectives vis-à-vis the United States or Western Europe. The USSR can, for example, assign some of its large medium-range bomber force for this purpose, station its early-model missile-firing submarines in the Pacific within range of the Chinese mainland, or allocate a few hundred ICBMs and IRBMs to the task of deterring China.

Thus, the Soviet Union would appear to have no serious need to increase its programmed strategic forces in order to deter China; indeed, it probably already possesses the weapons necessary for this purpose. Although the Soviet Union will be able to retain a significant damage limiting capacity against China, it would be virtually impossible for the USSR to acquire a reliable damage denial capability against China, given the variety of systems China could bring to bear against the Soviet homeland. The SALT accords will not adversely affect the Soviet deterrent capabilities against China and could even improve them, because the accords limit U.S. systems. In any event, any steps that the Russians might take to improve their deterrent capabilities against China would probably involve intermediate- and medium-range systems that would not threaten the United States or affect the provisions of the initial SALT agreement.

Consequently, there is no reason to believe that the growth of China's nuclear capabilities will create unmanageable problems for strategic stability or call into question the effectiveness of the nuclear deterrence concept that forms the basis for U.S. and Soviet strategic force plans. A Sino-Soviet nuclear conflict would increase, as would a Sino-American conflict, the risk of a U.S.–Soviet strategic exchange, but the hot line and accidental launch agreements between Washington and Moscow reduce the likelihood of such an event. In general, continuing contacts between the United States and the USSR in SALT and elsewhere should help to minimize the risk of future conflicts being generated by the triangular strategic relationship.

Extended Deterrence

Although it is highly probable that Chinese leaders will be deterred from using or threatening to use nuclear weapons and will also continue to be cautious in the use of conventional forces beyond China's borders, the growing Chinese nuclear force will, nevertheless, significantly change the environment in which the United States pursues its security policies in East Asia. It will thus affect the way in which the United States responds to situations in which military force might conceivably be used, and may also affect the attitude of its allies toward the United States.

Possible Inhibitions on the United States

China's possession of a growing nuclear force will create a possibility, at least, that the United States could be more inhibited and the Chinese less so than in the past in situations of confrontation and rising tension between the two nations. The United States might be more inhibited because it could not be certain it could prevent the damage the Chinese would have the nuclear capability to inflict on the United States or its allies. The Chinese might be inclined to take stronger action than they would have in the past, because they would believe, with some justification, that the United States would be more inhibited than toward a non-nuclear China.

It is difficult to predict how future U.S. or Chinese leaders would react to such hypothetical situations. The mere existence of Chinese nuclear forces and the possibility that such weapons might be launched, perhaps even inadvertently, would probably impose additional restraints on U.S. behavior. It seems probable, however, that while the United States would be more cautious than before China had nuclear weapons, China would be no less cautious than it has been. Chinese leaders could not be certain of their judgment as to how the United States would react, and the cost of a mistaken judgment would be so high that they would probably wish to have a wide margin of safety.

In addition to the caution that Peking's overall military inferiority would impose on China's behavior in general, the risk of provoking U.S. nuclear strikes would undoubtedly continue to constrain Peking from undertaking action that would lead to a serious military confrontation with the United States. From the viewpoint of a conservative Chinese planner, it will appear credible for some time to come (at least until the end of the seventies) that the United States could launch an attack that might completely destroy China's nuclear forces, simply by using existing U.S. strategic weapons; and complete reliance on a "launch-on-warning" policy to prevent the destruction of Chinese strategic delivery systems might be seen as technically uncertain and risky. Consequently, even though China does not need to acquire a highly reliable and effective nuclear force to satisfy its minimum deterrent objectives, China's nuclear force will not be sufficient in the 1970s to allow its leaders to take significantly greater risks than in the past in using or threatening to use military force outside its borders.[10]

In short, the net effect of China's possession of nuclear weapons is likely to be to make both the United States and China quite cautious about allowing a confrontation to grow to the point where there is a high risk of a large-scale direct clash between their military forces. Both would have a strong interest in finding ways to defuse such a rising spiral of action and reaction before it got out of hand. The efforts made by the United States and China to improve relations between them, symbolized by President Nixon's visit to China, reflect the increased interest both countries have, as two nuclear powers, in avoiding military conflict. (Of course, both countries have other, nonmilitary reasons to pursue this détente.) To the extent that this effort is successful and means are found to resolve conflicts of interest by negotiation rather than confrontation, the relative military power of the two countries will recede into the background as a factor in their relationship.

10. This conclusion is also drawn by Harry Gelber in "Nuclear Weapons in Chinese Strategy," *Problems of Communism*, vol. 20 (November–December 1971), pp. 33–34.

Effect on U.S. Allies

In addition to affecting the behavior of the United States and China in situations of heightened tension, the existence of the Chinese nuclear force might also affect both nuclear proliferation and relations between the United States and its allies. Where U.S. bases and forces are present in regions vulnerable to Chinese nuclear attack, U.S. allies might tend to question the reliability of the United States' nuclear guarantees if doubts should grow about the willingness of the United States to involve itself in any major military conflict with China. China's deployment of an ICBM system, which would bring U.S. territory under threat of attack, would accentuate such a tendency. Some of our allies could conceivably question the desirability of maintaining security ties with the United States or permitting American bases to remain on their territory for fear of becoming nuclear targets. Peking might try to encourage such tendencies in an attempt to weaken the U.S. network of alliances, to force the United States to remove its bases from Asia, or to obtain favorable settlements on key issues such as those relating to Taiwan and Korea. The confidence that the United States' allies have in its defense commitment will, of course, depend on the general state of relations with them. The existence of the Chinese nuclear force is only one factor in a complex equation, and it could be negated by effective U.S. policies toward the ally concerned. It must be recognized, however, that Chinese possession of nuclear weapons might be harmful to our alliance relationships and that U.S. policies will have to be shaped with this possibility in mind.

For the time being, and perhaps for a long period ahead, the nature of the triangular relationship among the Soviet Union, China, and the United States has eased the pressure that Chinese possession of nuclear weapons might otherwise have placed on the U.S. alliance system in Asia. The process now under way of expanding and improving relations between the United States and China both diminishes the military importance to the United States of its alliance system and decreases the threat that China once felt from it. The greater the momentum of the rapprochement between the United States and China, the more the U.S. alliance system will fade in importance as a military means of "containing" China. If, some years hence, there should be a marked decrease in hostility between the Soviet Union and China and a renewed U.S.–Chinese military confrontation, the United States would have to review the validity for the defense of its interests in the late 1970s or '80s of an alliance system constructed in the 1950s.

Finally, the existence of the Chinese nuclear force might have the effect of furthering nuclear proliferation. Japan, India, and Australia are all capable of producing nuclear weapons during the 1970s should they decide that such weapons were necessary for their security. But the fact that the Chinese would find their own security diminished if any of these powers, especially Japan, went nuclear will probably inhibit them from brandishing their nuclear weapons. The risk of proliferation will be further minimized if the United States and the Soviet Union also refrain from military policies and public statements that tend to magnify the importance of China's nuclear capacity.

Guidelines for U.S. Defense Policies

As the foregoing discussion suggests, a deterrence-based policy, supplemented by the damage limitation capabilities inherent in planned U.S. strategic forces, will be sufficient to deter or counter major Chinese aggressive acts without undermining positive U.S. foreign policy and arms control objectives vis-à-vis China or damaging U.S. relations with its Asian allies, notably Japan. It would be neither necessary nor desirable to seek to improve U.S. damage limitation options. Whatever potentially adverse effects the Chinese nuclear force might have on U.S. interests—through increased Chinese military power and political influence or limited U.S. freedom of action in dealing with China—cannot be negated by U.S. strategic weapons decisions. These effects can, however, be minimized by maintaining adequate conventional forces and giving effective assistance to our major allies, while at the same time pursuing policies aimed at reducing the risk of armed conflict with China.

Strategic Policies

While the United States should realistically acknowledge and adjust to the fact of Chinese nuclear capabilities, it would not be advisable to overstate the effectiveness of the Chinese nuclear force by suggesting that the United States might be deterred from using nuclear weapons or even from committing large-scale conventional military forces in the event of a conflict with China. Though it could be argued that such a course might reduce Chinese fears of U.S. aggression and thereby enhance prospects for arms control, it might also enable Peking to profit unduly in terms of prestige and influence from its small nuclear capability, as well as having an adverse effect on U.S. alliance relations. If other nations—Japan, in particular—were to conclude that even a small and vulnerable nuclear force not only can provide deterrence but also gives a nation great political influence, their interest in acquiring nuclear weapons would be heightened. While U.S. attitudes toward China's nuclear force will not be the decisive factor in other nations' decisions on whether to go nuclear, the United States should try to avoid actions that would add weight to the arguments of those favoring such action.

The United States should, therefore, adopt a middle course, accepting the fact that the Chinese will acquire a limited deterrent capacity but seeking to maintain confidence in the U.S. ability to protect its interests, fulfill its commitments, and respond if necessary to aggressive threats. The United States should make no threats of a first strike, and it should consider making a no-first-use pledge if real progress can be made toward other arms control measures and if appropriate conditions can be met (see the discussion in Chapter 5). In planning its forces, the U.S. goal should be to maintain effective deterrence without destabilizing U.S.–Soviet relations. Thus, the United States should not add to or improve its offensive forces simply to obtain greater damage limiting capabilities against China.

Finally, while the United States should treat China as a major power and seek to initiate an arms control dialogue with it, we should be wary of appearing to treat China with greater respect and deference because of its nuclear force. In particular, the United States must not allow its attempts to improve relations with China and initiate arms control discussions with Peking to damage vital relations with Japan or the Soviet Union. This proposed U.S. strategic policy should be sufficient to satisfy our interests vis-à-vis Japan so long as our regional defense capabilities and overall political relations with Japan are such as to preserve the credibility of our commitment to help defend Japan.

Regional Defense Posture

In addition to adjusting its strategic policies toward China in the ways suggested above, the United States should examine its defense posture in Asia as a whole in light of the impact of China's nuclear force and our desire to improve relations with the Chinese. This requires, above all, a hard look at the extent to which the United States should rely on strategic and tactical nuclear weapons to provide a capability to defend its interests against possible Chinese conventional attacks in the region. It can be shown that there are strong reasons for maintaining conventional forces powerful enough to meet conceivable contingencies without having to rely on nuclear weapons.

First, the political costs of being the first to use nuclear weapons in Asia would be extremely high—in all probability unacceptable—with global as well as regional repercussions and long-run as well as immediate consequences. It is difficult to visualize scenarios of conflict in which it would be in our interest to undertake the first use of nuclear weapons, either tactical or strategic, in Asia. Even our closest allies would oppose heavy U.S. dependence on nuclear weapons for their defense, in part because the idea of the United States using nuclear weapons against fellow Asians is repugnant, and in part because any actual use of nuclear weapons would increase the danger of devastation of their own territory.

Second, substantial reliance by the United States on the possible use of nuclear weapons against China or Chinese forces could increase the risk that in a crisis the Chinese would carry out a nuclear strike against U.S. allies or forces, or even against the United States itself (once the Chinese have ICBMs). This risk will grow as the Chinese nuclear force becomes larger and more sophisticated, until they acquire a reliable second-strike capability.

Third, substantial reliance on nuclear weapons to meet conventional attacks could tend to weaken our deterrent posture in Asia, since the possible use of nuclear weapons against China would become less credible as the Chinese improved their regional and long-range nuclear capabilities. The effect on the Japanese of such a policy could be especially detrimental to U.S. interests. Should U.S. conventional forces located in East Asia or available for use there be reduced below the level the Japanese government regards as justified by potential threats, the Japanese would become increasingly skeptical of U.S. willingness to use military force in situations where nuclear weapons might be our only option. This would tend to increase pressures in Japan to expand their own conventional forces and eventually acquire nuclear weapons in order to feel less at the mercy of nuclear-armed China and the USSR.

For all these reasons, it would be extremely unrealistic and risky for the United States to rely heavily in its strategic planning on the use of nuclear weapons against possible conventional action in Asia by Chinese or other forces. An American president should not be placed in a position in which he would only have two choices: the first use of nuclear weapons in Asia, with all the damage that would do to the U.S. position in the world, or acquiescing in serious damage to U.S. interests in Asia. Instead, the United States should be prepared to defend its vital interests and essential commitments in Asia against possible conventional attack with conventional forces—our own and those of our allies. It should draw down its conventional forces in East Asia only to the extent that this can be justified by improved relations and diminished risk of war with China and the USSR and does not impair Japanese confidence in the U.S. defense commitment to Japan. An assessment of current trends in East Asia, including the threats to states that the United States is committed to help defend, suggests that reliance on U.S. conventional forces to meet possible attacks by Chinese or other conventional forces is a realistic policy, even in the post-Vietnam climate of opinion in the United States.

Under the Nixon doctrine, the United States has reduced the size of its general purpose forces in Asia. This strategy is based on the assumptions that simultaneous conventional attacks against Europe and Asia are unlikely, that our principal long-term interests in Asia lie in Northeast Asia, that we will maintain existing U.S. defense commitments, that our Asian allies can and will improve their conventional defense capabilities, and that U.S. air- and sea-power will remain in the area.

Under current post-Vietnam planning, the United States would maintain four divisions committed to Asia—one based in the United States, one in South Korea (which is likely in time to be reduced below division size), and the others in Hawaii and Okinawa; tactical aircraft squadrons stationed in Korea, Okinawa, and the Philippines; and naval forces of the Seventh Fleet in the western Pacific. (The United States is also reported to be planning to retain tactical nuclear weapons on carriers in the Seventh Fleet and on delivery systems stationed in South Korea, Guam, and the Philippines.[11])

Most of our principal allies—including Japan, Australia, New Zealand, and the Philippines—are beyond the reach of any conventional force that China could create within the 1970s. Chinese conventional

11. "Symington Terms Some A-Weapons in Asia Insecure," *New York Times*, Jan. 19, 1971; "Little Strategic Loss Seen in Pullout from Taiwan," ibid., Aug. 16, 1971.

attacks against nations not allied to the United States, such as India, would of course be of concern to us; but in the absence of a formal U.S. defense commitment it could not be persuasively argued that a Chinese attack on such a country should affect the question of U.S. reliance on nuclear weapons in its defense planning for Asia. The areas in Asia where Chinese conventional attacks are conceivable and where the United States does have commitments affecting its force planning are Southeast Asia, Taiwan, and Korea. It is with respect to these areas that decisions must be made as to the size of U.S. conventional forces needed and the degree to which the United States should rely on nuclear weapons.

SOUTHEAST ASIA. Very large conventional forces would be needed to meet a full-scale Chinese attack on Thailand, to which the United States has a defense commitment. It might be argued that because of the great cost of maintaining such forces the United States should rely increasingly on nuclear power to deter aggression in this region. But it is difficult to make a convincing case that the United States has interests in Southeast Asia important enough to justify incurring the high costs and risks of the first use of nuclear weapons. President Nixon's public pledge not to use nuclear weapons—including tactical nuclear weapons—in Indochina suggests that their use anywhere in Southeast Asia is neither a credible nor a desirable foundation for U.S. policy or force planning. Given the remoteness of the possibility of a Chinese conventional attack in Southeast Asia, the United States need neither rely on nuclear weapons to deter such an attack nor maintain a conventional force for that purpose. Should Chinese policies change so radically as to make invasion of Southeast Asia a serious danger, the United States would have considerable warning time to modify appropriately its force levels and deployments, seek Soviet and Japanese collaboration in deterring Chinese aggression, or disengage from the defense commitment if U.S. interests no longer appeared to justify maintaining it.

TAIWAN. It is apparent that at present the Chinese do not have the capability to mount a major conventional attack across the Taiwan Strait against the conventional defenses they could expect to encounter, and it is doubtful that they could even mount a successful attack against the offshore islands. Peking's amphibious capabilities are minimal, the Nationalist air force is fairly strong, and U.S. conventional air and sea power could be called on from bases elsewhere in Asia or the Pacific if necessary. Moreover, the risk of a clash with Peking over Taiwan has been substantially reduced by the implicit understanding between President Nixon and Chou En-lai reflected in the Shanghai communiqué,[12] and by the progress made since then in improving U.S. relations with China.

KOREA. Korea presents more complicated and difficult problems than the other two areas. It is of great importance to the United States because developments there could have severe repercussions on the vital U.S. relationship with Japan. Despite the strength of the well-armed South Korean forces and the U.S. conventional forces in the area, a massive North Korean attack with large-scale Chinese participation might be difficult to handle with confidence by conventional forces alone. Yet the military and political risks of relying on nuclear weapons, especially tactical nuclear weapons based in South Korea, to meet a conventional attack in the Korean peninsula are very high. First use of tactical nuclear weapons by the United States against a conventional attack could provoke the use of tactical nuclear weapons by the Soviet Union (or by China when it has such weapons), largely canceling out the military advantage of the U.S. initiative and multiplying destruction in Korea. First use of nuclear weapons by the United States would shock the Japanese, calling into question whether they would permit the continued use of U.S. bases in Japan to defend Korea. The United States would, in addition, incur all the political costs associated with the use of nuclear weapons against Asians.

So long as the Chinese remain concerned about the Soviet threat and consequently desire reasonably good relations with the United States, they are most unlikely to participate in a conflict in Korea. In any case, the presence of U.S. conventional forces in Korea would serve as a strong deterrent. Stationing U.S. tactical nuclear weapons on South Korean territory can add only marginally to this deterrent effect, for the Chinese are aware that the United States could quickly bring nuclear weapons from outside Korea into action on a Korean battlefield. In addition to all the other disadvantages of the deployment of U.S. tactical nuclear weapons in Korea, their presence would cause U.S. military planners to rely unduly on their possible use in an emergency.

Unless there should be an extreme deterioration in U.S.–Chinese relations, the U.S. forces now stationed in South Korea should be adequate to meet any conceivable contingencies. Although further improve-

12. Ibid., Feb. 28, 1972.

ment in U.S.–Chinese relations would justify a further reduction of these forces, reductions should not be based on heavier dependence on nuclear weapons. In order to make the situation in Korea less dangerous and reduce the need for large forces there, the United States should explore the possibility of international agreements regarding Korea.[13]

This review of the contingencies in Asia that might call for U.S. military intervention against a Chinese attack suggests that the current level of U.S. forces committed to Asia should be adequate at least through the 1970s, barring serious deterioration in U.S.–Chinese relations or a radical change in Chinese reluctance to use their forces beyond their borders. It suggests also that the United States should reduce its reliance on tactical nuclear weapons wherever, as in Korea, the military and political costs and risks of using them against conventional attack are likely to outweigh any possible advantages. Finally, it suggests that further conventional force reductions should depend on a diminishing risk of war with China and the USSR, rather than on greater reliance on nuclear weapons. U.S. forces on Taiwan can be safely reduced and ultimately removed in order to help reduce tensions. It would be inadvisable, however, for political as well as military reasons, to withdraw all U.S. forces from Korea—at least until North-South tensions had declined sufficiently for South Korea to concur in this action or until international agreements could be achieved.[14] Care should be taken that any further U.S. force reductions do not undermine Japanese confidence in the U.S. defense commitment to Japan.

Although the Chinese have consistently demanded the withdrawal of U.S. forces from East Asia and the dismantling of U.S. bases in the region, they are not at present pressing for the withdrawal of U.S. forces from any part of East Asia except Taiwan, because of their fear of Soviet expansionism and the military threat it poses to China. Present Chinese leaders appear to feel that the presence of U.S. forces serves as a useful counter to the Soviet Union; they do not wish the USSR to have the most visible conventional forces in the western Pacific. Moreover, there is some evidence that the Chinese fear that Japan might be tempted to undertake a military role in South Korea if U.S. forces there were totally withdrawn. Consequently, the Chinese might well prefer the continued

13. See Chapter 6.
14. Issues involved in planning U.S. regional forces are analyzed by Leslie Gelb and Arnold Kuzmack in "General Purpose Forces," in Henry Owen (ed.), *The Next Phase in Foreign Policy* (Brookings Institution, 1973), pp. 203–24.

presence of strong U.S. conventional forces in the western Pacific rather than heavy U.S. reliance on nuclear weapons. The latter alternative would be a less effective counter to Soviet conventional forces and might also appear to heighten the danger to China in the event of renewed tension with the United States.[15]

In a fundamental sense, U.S. security interests in Asia can best be furthered through the improvement of U.S.–Chinese relations, the development of a more stable military balance in Asia, and international cooperation in the arms control field. In order to facilitate progress toward greater regional stability and improve the chances of involving China in arms control measures, the United States should be sensitive to possible Chinese reactions to U.S. defense decisions and try to avoid policies and actions that might appear provocative to the Chinese. Such a posture would call for lowering the U.S. nuclear profile in Asia and minimizing the conventional forces deployed close to China's borders.

Conclusions

The nuclear weapons that China will possess within the 1970s probably will not require heavy new defense burdens for the United States. Strategic weapons already existing or planned to meet the requirements of the strategic balance with the Soviet Union should be adequate to deter China also. It would be unnecessary and undesirable to add to or improve weapons or equipment solely in order to increase the U.S. damage limitation capability against China.

The principal effects that Chinese nuclear weapons will have on U.S. defense policies will be to create a need for measures to reduce the risk of accidental or unauthorized launching of nuclear missiles, to make the United States more cautious in handling situations that could result in military confrontation with China, and to require actions by the United States to counter possible damage to the credibility of U.S. defense commitments to its allies. To maintain this credibility, the United States should avoid overstating the effectiveness of the Chinese nuclear force and should reduce its dependence on nuclear weapons to deter or

15. Hsieh suggests that the Chinese might interpret the Nixon doctrine not merely as a welcome U.S. disengagement, but as possibly leading to a Japanese arms buildup or greater U.S. reliance on nuclear weapons (*ABM, MIRV, SALT, and the Nuclear Arms Race*, Hearings, p. 138).

defend against possible Chinese attack. This will require the mainte-
nance of adequate conventional forces for possible use in Northeast
Asia in order to preserve Japanese confidence in the United States and
thus to avoid increased risk of nuclear proliferation. The present level of
conventional forces appears adequate for this purpose, and this level
can be further reduced if U.S. and Japanese relations with China continue to improve and tensions in East Asia further decline.

CHAPTER THREE

China's Nuclear Weapons and Arms Control

The growth of China's nuclear delivery capabilities raises a variety of questions about the future stability and efficacy of the Strategic Arms Limitation Talks (SALT) agreements, the nonproliferation treaty (NPT), and other existing nuclear arms control agreements. It also affects the prospects for negotiating additional multilateral measures, such as a comprehensive nuclear test ban (CTB), during the 1970s. Particularly important is the possible impact of China on nuclear arms control; to date arms control efforts have centered on weapons of mass destruction, and China, which is now acquiring such weapons, maintains that in any disarmament effort nuclear weapons are of paramount importance.

Implications for SALT

In late 1969, after almost three years of preparatory efforts, the United States and the USSR initiated talks on the subject of strategic arms limitations. The decision to treat this issue bilaterally and outside of existing multilateral forums was based on the fact that no other nation possessed nuclear arsenals of the same magnitude as the two superpowers. It also reflected the judgment that negotiations on these complex and crucial questions could best be treated at this stage in private discussions between Washington and Moscow. Participation by Britain, France, and China—all of which have only small strategic nuclear capabilities—did not seem vital to the success of initial U.S.–Soviet strategic limitation arrangements.

In the spring of 1972, after more than three years of SALT negotia-

48

tions, the United States and the Soviet Union agreed to restrict anti-ballistic missiles (ABMs) to two sites and 200 interceptors on each side and to freeze the number of intercontinental ballistic missiles (ICBMs) and submarine-launched ballistic missiles (SLBMs) on both sides at existing levels for a five-year period.[1] By a later agreement, the number of ABMs allowed each side was reduced to 100 missiles at one site. In October 1974, it was agreed at Vladivostok to negotiate an agreement to last through December 1985 that would place equal ceilings of 2,400 on the total number of ICBMs, SLBMs, and long-range bombers each side can have, with sub-ceilings of 1,320 for the number of missiles armed with multiple independently targetable reentry vehicles (MIRVs).

Effect of SALT Agreements on U.S. Ability to Deter China

Under the SALT agreements negotiated thus far, the United States can retain all its tactical and theater nuclear forces and sufficient strategic capabilities to maintain an effective deterrent against China as well as the Soviet Union. Indeed, because the agreements permit the United States to implement all the strategic programs now planned while limiting Soviet as well as American ABMs and offensive missiles, a greater proportion of U.S. strategic warheads will be available for contingencies relating to China than would otherwise be the case. Given the projected growth of China's nuclear forces, the United States will also continue to have a substantial offensive damage limitation capability against China throughout the 1970s.

The United States and the USSR plan to continue their SALT negotiations with a view to reaching agreements on reductions of strategic delivery vehicles and possibly placing some restrictions on weapons improvements, such as constraints on improvements in missile accuracy. But it is doubtful that during the seventies it will be feasible for the superpowers to agree on large reductions in force levels, meaningful qualitative limitation, or even prohibitions against replacing existing strategic systems with more advanced ones. Thus, even future SALT agreements are not likely to detract from U.S. deterrent capabilities against China.

As the USSR acquires increasing survival capability from the deployment of SLBMs, and to the extent that the U.S.–Soviet strategic relationship is stabilized by additional SALT agreements, it will become less

1. See *The ABM Treaty and the Interim Agreement*, Message by President Richard M. Nixon to the Congress, June 13, 1972.

and less practical for the United States to seek damage limitation capabilities against the USSR. On the other hand, present U.S. strategic plans and programs call for developing a capacity to attack Soviet ICBM sites in order to be able to match any counterforce weapons the USSR may develop. Whatever the outcome of this ongoing U.S.–Soviet interaction, conservative planning within the framework of the SALT agreements will ensure that the United States has forces adequate to deter China from using nuclear weapons, without the necessity of acquiring additional weapons specifically for this purpose.

In formulating the SALT agreements, U.S. and Soviet leaders considered all relevant aspects of their security needs, including the requirements of their defense and foreign policy postures toward Peking and the possible effects of the accords on other "Nth countries" (that is, countries capable of acquiring nuclear weapons). Although the agreements concluded obviously satisfied the present strategic requirements relating to China, of both sides, the shape of the accords was primarily determined by each nation's strategic requirements vis-à-vis each other; the need to ensure a continuing capability to deal with China was apparently only a secondary consideration. That the sub-ceiling on MIRVed missiles established at Vladivostok, for example, was so high was largely due to problems of verification, definition, and asymmetries that have little relevance to China's nuclear force. Of particular importance to the USSR is the fact that the SALT agreements place no restrictions on Soviet medium-range missiles and bombers that can be used to deter China and to deal as well with Britain and France—two additional nuclear powers in range of the USSR.

One desirable side effect of the severe limitations on ABMs—a provision that reflects primarily the desire to maximize bilateral U.S.–Soviet stability—will be to prevent the United States from choosing a strategic option that would have undesirable consequences for U.S. relations with China. Were it not for the SALT agreements, the United States might well have decided to build a nationwide Safeguard ABM system. Administration leaders were initially in favor of an "anti-Chinese" ABM system but, as the SALT talks progressed, modified this position in the interest of negotiating an agreement with the USSR.[2]

2. In his January 30, 1970, press conference, President Nixon claimed that an area ABM was "essential" to U.S. diplomacy in Asia but implied that the United States might conceivably reverse its policy in the future if relations between Washington and Peking improved. In justifying the ABM treaty, U.S. officials argued that the gain in U.S.–Soviet stability was worth the loss of an anti-Chinese ABM.

It is possible, of course, that Congress might have continued to deny funds for an area ABM system or that the administration itself might have concluded eventually that such a system was unnecessary, impractical, or injurious to U.S.–Soviet as well as U.S.–Chinese relations. However, this is by no means certain, and, in the absence of a SALT accord (and assuming the continued growth of the Chinese force and the probable expansion of Soviet ABMs), a nationwide deployment of an area ABM system might well have taken place.

The initial SALT agreement commits the United States and the USSR not to construct nationwide ABM defenses. This will prevent both nations from deploying anti-Chinese ABMs of the Sentinel or full Safeguard types, as long as the treaty is observed. Such a system would have required something on the order of 1,000 interceptors and a network of large radars. Apart from the fact that such a system would not be desirable from the viewpoint of U.S. policies toward China, it could also adversely affect U.S.–Soviet relations and disrupt the stability of any SALT arrangement. In any event, it would be extremely difficult to reach agreement on how to define or design nationwide ABM systems for both nations in ways that would take into account the technological and geographic asymmetries between them.

It should be noted that the Russians seem to be prepared to forgo an anti-Chinese ABM—possibly because they realize that a really effective ABM defense against China's mix of medium-range missiles and aircraft would be virtually impossible to achieve—and that they reportedly opposed the idea of deploying "thin" nationwide ABM systems on an agreed basis as part of a SALT treaty.

Importance of Chinese Participation in SALT

For some years to come there will be no compelling reasons to try to bring the Chinese into the SALT forum, nor is it likely that they would soon be interested in joining. At least throughout the 1970s, the absence of the Chinese in a SALT agreement will pose no serious problems for U.S. defense policies or for our strategic arms control objectives, since China's nuclear force will not yet have approached levels that would make Chinese participation essential for U.S.–Soviet stability. Moreover, the addition of a third party to SALT—even if that party were not deliberately obstructionist, which could not be taken for granted in the case of China—would further complicate what are already exceedingly complex negotiations.

The Chinese have not shown any interest in joining the SALT negotiations. On the contrary, they have denounced SALT agreements as
collusion between the superpowers, referred to them as sham agreements that simply codify the nuclear arms race, accused the United
States and the Soviet Union of building up their armaments while insisting that other nations forgo nuclear weapons, and reiterated their call
for a world disarmament conference, for no-first-use pledges, and other
steps toward total disarmament.[3]

There is some validity to the Chinese position, of course, aside from
whatever political advantages they may see in opposing all limited arms
control measures initiated by the two superpowers. Although China
benefits from the banning of nationwide "anti-Chinese" ABM systems,
the SALT agreements will not reduce in any meaningful way the nuclear capabilities in relation to China of the U.S. or Soviet strategic
offensive systems, Moscow's medium-range missile systems, or U.S. or
Soviet tactical nuclear weapons. And the limited measures likely to be
negotiated in the next phases of SALT will probably not seriously restrict U.S. or Soviet counterforce capabilities against China. To date,
moreover, there has been no indication that SALT will produce no-first-
use pledges by Washington or Moscow.

Not only has China denounced the SALT agreements between the
United States and the USSR, but, immediately after exploding its first
nuclear device, it officially opposed the concept of controlling or reducing delivery systems.[4] Peking's position on this matter may to some
extent reflect a lack of understanding of the potential benefits of limited
arms control agreements in general, but it must also reflect Chinese
awareness of the realities of China's strategic inferiority. Indeed, some
of the Chinese objections to proposals to limit strategic delivery systems
have displayed a fairly sophisticated awareness of the inherent difficulties in negotiating these measures, such as the problems posed by "conventional" aircraft. It may be, therefore, that not until the Chinese
acquire a reasonably credible deterrent—perhaps in the 1980s—will
they see compelling reasons to participate in steps to limit strategic
deployments.

3. See speech by Chou En-lai of July 17, 1972; reported in Foreign Broadcast
Information Service (FBIS), *Daily Report: People's Republic of China,* July 18,
1972, p. A3. See also speech by Vice Foreign Minister Chiao Kuan-hua on Oct. 3,
1972, at the United Nations General Assembly outlining China's general position on
disarmament (reported in ibid., Oct. 6, 1972, pp. A7–A10).

4. Morton Halperin, *China and the Bomb* (Praeger, 1965), pp. 126–29.

Nonetheless, there are disadvantages to Peking's absence from discussions on strategic arms limitations. For instance, the anticipated deployment of Chinese ICBMs will heighten the problem of accidental or unauthorized missile launchings, at least from the U.S. viewpoint. U.S. and Soviet negotiators used the framework of SALT to reach collateral agreements on improved hot line communication in crisis situations and other steps to diminish the dangers of accidental nuclear war. It would also be useful for the United States and the USSR—and this could also involve China—to seek ways of avoiding the interference with satellite reconnaissance systems that might create serious misunderstandings.

As China's nuclear force grows it will become increasingly important for the United States and the USSR to find ways of discussing with China the problems of limiting the further increase of strategic nuclear weapons. Perhaps by the early 1980s the increase in size of China's nuclear force will have encouraged the Chinese to take part in multilateral talks. It might then be possible to expand SALT to include not only China but also Britain and France.

In the meantime, however, it does not seem desirable to press for China to join the SALT negotiations. Bilateral discussions between the United States and China and the Soviet Union and China are likely to prove more practicable than the multilateral forum as a means of drawing the Chinese into serious consideration of the problems of strategic nuclear forces.[5] Some discussion between the United States and the USSR of the implications of the Chinese nuclear force could also be desirable.

The Geneva Talks

Up until now China has shown no interest in participating in the Conference of the Committee on Disarmament (CCD) or any other arms control forum except a world disarmament conference of all nations—and that only if all nuclear powers (especially the Soviet Union and the United States) first pledge not to use nuclear weapons against each other or against nonnuclear countries, and, in addition, withdraw all their forces and military bases from foreign countries.[6] In December

5. See Chapter 4 for a discussion of bilateral U.S. approaches to China.
6. Speech by Vice Foreign Minister Chiao Kuan-hua at UNGA, Oct. 3, 1972; reported in FBIS, *Daily Report: People's Republic of China*, Oct. 6, 1972, pp. A-9, A-10.

1973, however, China voted for the draft resolution of the United Nations General Assembly that established a forty-nation ad hoc committee to examine the views of governments on convening a world disarmament conference, and the Chinese then agreed to maintain contact with that committee, while still reiterating their previously stated conditions for holding such a conference.[7]

Greater Chinese experience in the United Nations may in time convince Peking that participation in the CCD would serve its interests better than remaining on the outside and condemning its activities. While Chinese participation at Geneva could create new problems, and possibly complicate the task of achieving agreements in that forum, their continued refusal to participate might have even more serious adverse effects. On balance, therefore, it is desirable to induce China to join. For this to happen, there will clearly have to be some changes in the organizational structure of the Geneva talks. In particular, the United States and Soviet Union will probably have to accept some new arrangement regarding the chairmanship, such as a rotating chairmanship. In bilateral arms control discussions with China, then, the United States should make clear its willingness to consider and discuss the question of Chinese participation in the CCD.

Nonproliferation

Of the five states with nuclear weapons, only China and France have thus far refused to accede to the nuclear nonproliferation treaty. France has indicated, however, that it will act as if it had signed the treaty and will assume all the obligations placed on nuclear powers. China has opposed the NPT and refused to endorse explicitly the goal of nonproliferation. This policy and the continued growth of China's nuclear force raise questions about the effectiveness of the NPT in curbing the spread of nuclear weapons to countries such as India and Israel, that have not signed the treaty, or Japan and the UAR, that have signed but not ratified the accord.

7. Speeches by Chinese representatives Chuang Yen and An Chih-yuan at UNGA, Dec. 13, 1973, and Nov. 4, 1974; reported in ibid., Dec. 17, 1973, pp. A-4, A-5 and Nov. 4, 1974, pp. A6–A9.

Effect of China's Nuclear Force

The growth of Chinese nuclear capabilities might in itself, under some circumstances, make certain nations reluctant to ratify the NPT or more prone to abrogate it in the future. The potential nuclear powers most affected by the increase in Chinese nuclear capabilities—Japan and India—would give more serious consideration to acquiring nuclear arms if they perceived an increased Chinese threat to themselves or if they concluded that the Chinese were reaping important political benefits from their nuclear weapons and decided that it was impossible to gain the prestige and influence of a major power without them. India's detonation of a nuclear device in May 1974, although allegedly for the purpose of developing nuclear explosives for peaceful uses, was clearly related to such considerations. Prospects for proliferation would be increased by greater Chinese aggressiveness or a tendency of the United States or the Soviet Union to defer to China because of its added nuclear capacity. But there are strong economic, political, and military arguments against the acquisition of nuclear weapons by either India or Japan and the Chinese seem unlikely to adopt the high-risk military strategy or aggressive foreign policy that would precipitate such events. Furthermore, there are other important potentially nuclear nations, such as Israel, that will be only marginally affected by the Chinese nuclear force. On balance, therefore, the growth of China's nuclear force probably will not have significant adverse consequences for proliferation—except for the Indian detonation—just as there were few significant effects of China's entry into the nuclear club in 1964 or from the deployment of its first IRBMs in 1971. Even in Japan, there is no evidence today of widespread alarm at the fact that Tokyo is now a potential target of China's missiles.

Chinese Policies Regarding Proliferation

Historically, China's nonproliferation policy has not been a positive one, but neither has it been totally negative. Before detonating its first nuclear device, China denied that an increase in the number of nuclear nations would necessarily lead to an increased risk of nuclear war and claimed that bombs in the hands of socialist states would be advantageous. During 1965, as if to justify its own actions, Peking spoke of the importance of breaking the superpowers' monopoly, continued to claim that proliferation was inevitable, and expressed hope that the Afro-

Asian nations would be able to manufacture their own bombs. China's position, in short, was that further proliferation could be beneficial, rather than dangerous, and that it could even make total nuclear disarmament more rather than less likely to occur.[8]

When the NPT was being negotiated, Peking, consistent with its opposition to all limited multilateral arms control measures, called the treaty a fraud and accused the United States and the USSR of collaboration designed to discriminate against nonnuclear nations. It is true, of course, that from a security standpoint neither the NPT nor any of the arms control measures negotiated during the 1960s would have removed the regional threat to China or eliminated Peking's fear of possible nuclear attack by the United States or the USSR.

On the other hand, there is evidence suggesting that China is aware that nuclear proliferation is not, in fact, in China's interest. In practice, the Chinese have *not* provided nuclear weapons assistance to other nations; they are reported to have once turned down a request from the UAR for such aid.[9] Even when arguing the inevitability or the desirability of proliferation to friendly nations in the mid-1960s, Peking stated that it would be "unrealistic" for anyone to ask China for nuclear assistance. And in fact, Peking's arms control positions now tend to be consistent with the goal of nonproliferation. There is a significant sense in which China's strong advocacy of no-first-use pledges might be viewed as an antiproliferation policy designed both to persuade other nations of the limited utility of nuclear weapons and to diminish their fear of Chinese attack. The nuclear-free zones advocated by China could be regarded as "regional" nonproliferation schemes. Moreover, the Chinese have included the possibility of a nuclear nonacquisition agreement in their proposals for comprehensive nuclear disarmament.

Finally, China has not adopted a policy of nuclear threats and has not in fact attempted to use its nuclear weapons for aggressive purposes. Perhaps Peking's cautiousness has stemmed partly from the fear that a hostile policy could trigger proliferation decisions in other nations, notably Japan; China has already shown anxiety over the possibility that Japan might seek to acquire a nuclear capability, perhaps with U.S.

8. See M. H. Halperin and D. H. Perkins, *Communist China and Arms Control* (Harvard University, East Asian Research Center, 1965), for a discussion of China's arms control positions during the early 1960s.

9. Chalmers Roberts, "Will China Assume a New Sense of Responsibility?" *Washington Post*, Nov. 22, 1971. See also Mohamed Heikal, *The Cairo Documents* (Doubleday, 1973).

assistance. For example, in July 1971, Chou En-lai reportedly said that Japanese economic expansion must be followed by military expansion. Adding that Japan now claimed a "lifeline" that seemed to stretch from northeast China to the Malacca Straits, Chou said, "It is not possible to have such plans without including nuclear weapons."[10] In August 1971, he reiterated and elaborated on these views.[11]

The important question, of course, is what Peking's attitude toward proliferation is likely to be in the future. There is no immediate prospect for formal Chinese adherence to the NPT, and it is doubtful that China will even be willing to take a public position of opposition to further proliferation, at least in the near future. However, it seems highly probable that, over the next few years, China will increasingly come to recognize that the spread of nuclear weapons is *not* in its security interests. Peking can be expected to continue its policy of not providing nuclear weapons assistance to other nations, though it might consider assistance to others in the peaceful use of nuclear energy. Furthermore, concern over triggering decisions by other nations to go nuclear will probably continue to inhibit Peking from acting belligerently, even after the strength of its own nuclear forces has grown. It is even conceivable that China might mitigate its hostility toward the NPT in order to encourage adherence to the treaty by other states.

Peking will probably continue to show a strong interest in forestalling a Japanese decision to go nuclear.[12] China's basic fear of a militarized Japan, the very real concern that Japan could surpass China in a nuclear arms race and pose a serious security threat to Peking, and the possible reduction in Chinese political influence in Asia relative to Japan are all factors that will operate in this direction. China has sought to do what

10. In an interview with Australian Labor Party leader Gough Whitlam; see the *Washington Post*, July 7, 1971.

11. In an interview with James Reston, *New York Times*, Aug. 10, 1971.

12. The Chinese have frequently expressed concern over the danger of Japanese rearmament. Their expressions of concern mounted after the Nixon-Sato communiqué of November 1969, which declared Japan's interest in the security of South Korea and the Taiwan area. See, for example, the joint editorial of the *People's Daily* and the *Liberation Army Daily* of Sept. 3, 1970, and Mao's message to Kim Il-song on Sept. 8, 1970, both reported in *Peking Review*, Sept. 11, 1970, p. 8), and the Oct. 9, 1970, message from the Chinese Communist Party Central Committee to the North Korean United Workers' Party (ibid., Oct. 16, 1970, p. 3). With the improvement of relations between Peking and Washington and the establishment of diplomatic relations between Tokyo and Peking, Chinese attacks on "Japanese militarism" declined, but there is little doubt that Japan's military potential will continue to be cause for Chinese concern.

it can to strengthen antiwar factions in Japan, and Peking may well recognize that the U.S.–Japanese security relationship does lessen the prospects for a nuclear Japan. Though Chou En-lai once brushed this view aside as a "forced argument,"[13] he later reportedly acknowledged Japan's need to depend on the U.S. nuclear umbrella.[14]

India's breaching of the nonproliferation line that had stood for nearly a decade can hardly be welcome to China, given India's close association with the USSR and the possibility that the Indians may go on to produce nuclear weapons. The Indian detonation not only creates a new potential threat to Chinese security, but the Chinese must also fear that it will reduce Japanese inhibitions against a similar step. Decisions by Australia or other nations in Asia and the Pacific to go nuclear would further undermine China's efforts to exert its influence in that region. A nuclear weapons program initiated by a nation even as geographically remote from China as the UAR would not bring Peking any real benefits and might conceivably increase the danger of super-power clashes involving China.

On balance, therefore, Peking will probably come to recognize that widespread nuclear proliferation would endanger regional and international stability, tend to increase the costs for China of maintaining a deterrent against varied threats and "matching" other nations' forces, and increase the risk of accidental nuclear war. While Peking might foresee some benefits from the increased tension among other nations and the reduction of U.S. and Soviet influence that proliferation of nuclear weapons could cause, its judgment of the net effect of proliferation will probably be that, over the long term, it would be undesirable.

For this reason, the possibility of eventual Chinese support of the NPT should not be ruled out. Unlike agreements that limit nuclear testing or deployments, such as the test ban and SALT agreements, the NPT would place no restrictions on Chinese nuclear forces. Moreover, by signing the treaty Peking could reinforce its image as a responsible nuclear power and help ensure that nations such as Japan will remain nonnuclear. In the past, China has tended to oppose policy objectives that maintained the status quo in the world and has sought to draw a sharp line of demarcation between itself and the superpowers in order

13. In the interview with James Reston cited in note 10, above.
14. In an interview with Japanese Liberal Democratic leader Takeo Kimura, *Sankei* (Tokyo), Jan. 29, 1973.

to reinforce its role as champion of the Third World nations. But as China acquires a larger nuclear capability and assumes a greater international role it may find that strengthening the NPT by its adherence would serve its purposes better than remaining aloof. If China does at some point consider signing the NPT, however, it might demand concessions in other arms control areas—such as U.S. and Soviet no-first-use declarations—as a quid pro quo.

The continued buildup of China's nuclear force, combined with its nonadherence to the NPT, will not necessarily destroy the treaty's effectiveness or lead to further proliferation. If, for instance, all nonnuclear states joined the NPT, thus pledging not to receive nuclear weapons or assistance, any Chinese efforts to disrupt the treaty probably would not be very successful. Even if Peking, contrary to its past behavior, sought actively to transfer nuclear weapons or technology, potential recipients would be inhibited from accepting such aid not only by the legal obligations of the treaty, but also for fear of losing the benefits of peaceful nuclear energy programs or inviting reprisals or intervention by the United States or the USSR. In such a situation, however, there would still be the risk that a signatory nation might abrogate the treaty if it believed that an adversary was about to accept nuclear weapons from China. Over the long term, therefore, it would be useful, even though not essential, to obtain China's accession to the NPT in order to eliminate any possibility that China might aid other nations in circumventing it.

The more important and immediate problem raised by China's nuclear force, as suggested earlier, is that the Chinese might work against the possibility of getting all nonnuclear nations to sign and ratify the NPT in the next few years. Some nations that have either not signed or not ratified the treaty may have been encouraged to hold off by Peking's policy toward proliferation. Most such states would probably welcome Chinese adherence to the treaty or support of it and would then be somewhat more inclined to participate themselves—particularly if Chinese adherence or support were part of a broad pattern of positive policies toward limited nuclear arms control agreements. Nonetheless, continued routine Chinese declarations of opposition to the NPT probably would not severely damage prospects for additional states to sign or ratify the treaty, to judge from international reactions to Chinese denunciations of the limited test ban treaty. But if Peking were to adopt a policy of extreme hostility to the treaty, actively using its influence to induce other states not to sign or ratify, the prospects for nonproliferation could be seriously damaged, particularly if the Chinese were to revert to their earlier public position that it would be desirable for more nations to have nuclear weapons.

It is not anticipated that China will take such a course. What seems most likely in the period immediately ahead is that the Chinese will avoid taking an explicit stance on proliferation while continuing in practice a policy of not providing nuclear assistance. Though public support of nonproliferation by China may be too much to hope for in the near future, even a neutral stance could have some favorable effects (not least for Chinese interests) in making it easier for other nations to sign or ratify the treaty, and thereby contribute to the stability of the agreement.

Effect on Other Arms Control Measures

China's acquisition of a small nuclear force and its determination to expand it into a reliable deterrent shape its attitudes toward existing and proposed agreements for controlling nuclear arms. It is understandable that the Chinese should oppose agreements, such as the limited test ban treaty (LTB), that would place constraints on China that the superpowers did not have at a comparable stage in their nuclear development. But there are other existing or proposed agreements that could be participated in by China with little or no effect on its defense program. Chinese participation in arms control agreements is not crucial now to their acceptance by other nations, but prolonged refusal by China to take part in agreements or negotiations would eventually weaken support for at least some of them.

Test Ban

China sharply denounced the LTB while it was still being negotiated and after it was concluded in 1963. Peking claimed that the agreement represented U.S.–Soviet collusion to prevent other nations from conducting tests and acquiring nuclear weapons, and it sought to persuade other nations not to join. The Chinese pointed out that the treaty would not prevent the superpowers from continuing to test underground, developing new tactical as well as strategic nuclear weapons, and building up their arsenals. This position made sense, from Peking's viewpoint, when China was still in the early stages of developing and improving its own nuclear weapons. Moreover, Peking's conclusion that the LTB would not stop the United States and the USSR from enlarging and improving their nuclear forces has in fact proved to be correct. Given China's stance on nuclear proliferation, as well as its own stage of nuclear development, the argument that the LTB would inhibit the spread of nuclear weapons could obviously have no appeal for Peking. The Chinese may worry to some extent about the stigma of continuing to contribute to fallout, but not to the point of denying themselves the measures necessary to meet a perceived security need.

Obtaining China's participation in the LTB, even at this late stage, would be useful, though not crucial. Atmospheric testing can be considered to constitute a flagrant display of nuclear capabilities and disregard for the problems of fallout; many nonnuclear nations view it as both disturbing and threatening. China's accession to this treaty could, therefore, help to strengthen support for the NPT and increase the chance of its ratification by others. Chinese adherence might well put pressure on France to accede, or at least to refrain from atmospheric testing. If France and China both joined the LTB, additional "Nth countries" would be more strongly discouraged from entering the nuclear weapons club.

It is, of course, possible that during the 1970s China could reverse its position on atmospheric nuclear testing. For one thing, if the Chinese begin to develop a stronger interest in preventing proliferation, they might consider supporting the LTB with a view to strengthening it against possible abrogation by Japan or other states, since, as already noted, entry into the nuclear club through the use of underground testing would be more difficult than using atmospheric testing. Growing international political pressure against atmospheric testing could induce China to rethink its position, but it is unlikely that this would lead to a rapid reversal of Peking's position, even if the French were to stop atmospheric tests. However, as Peking deploys a larger nuclear force, gains additional data from its weapons tests, and acquires the technological capabilities that make underground testing less costly and difficult, Chinese leaders might reconsider their attitude toward the LTB. And even if they do not actually sign the treaty, they might simply decide unilaterally at some point to halt atmospheric testing.

China has denounced the proposed comprehensive test ban treaty (CTB) in terms similar to its position on the LTB. In his speech at the

United Nations on October 3, 1972, Chinese Vice Foreign Minister Chiao Kuan-hua declared that "a mere cessation of all nuclear tests without complete prohibition and thorough destruction of nuclear weapons can only hinder countries with few or no nuclear weapons from developing their nuclear capabilities for self-defense, but will not affect in the least the nuclear hegemony of the superpowers." He added that "China is ready at any time to stop all her nuclear tests, but only on the day the nuclear weapons of the nuclear superpowers and all nuclear countries are completely banned and thoroughly destroyed and not before."[15] China voted against all eight resolutions opposing nuclear testing that were considered by the United Nations in 1971, 1972, and 1973.[16] Again, this is an understandable position for a China still so far inferior to the United States and the USSR in nuclear weapons. And indeed, despite the size of their forces and the experience of over two decades of nuclear testing, the superpowers have not yet managed to agree on a comprehensive test ban.

China's future attitude toward a comprehensive ban may prove to be especially important to its success or failure. Peking's nonparticipation in a CTB would make its acceptance more difficult for the United States and the USSR, since opponents of the treaty could argue that the danger of a Chinese "nuclear breakthrough" could not be fully met by an escape clause in such an agreement. Furthermore, nonnuclear nations interested in placing further constraints on the nuclear powers will tend to react negatively to a CTB if Peking adopts a hostile attitude toward it. It is unfortunate that the CTB—the nuclear arms control agreement of possibly the greatest importance during the next few years—happens to be one of the measures *least likely* to be supported by China; in fact, in 1974 it voted against a UN resolution advocating a CTB. This will complicate both the problem of negotiating the agreement and the problem of trying to bring China into other arms control arrangements.

Although a comprehensive test ban could have benefits from China's point of view, these are not likely to be sufficient to convince Peking it

15. Quoted in FBIS, *Daily Report: People's Republic of China*, Oct. 6, 1972, p. A9. China also voted against the resolution adopted by the UN Conference on the Human Environment at Stockholm in June 1972, condemning and calling for an end to all nuclear tests, particularly those in the atmosphere (see ibid., June 16, 1972, p. A1).

16. For a useful summary of the positions on arms control taken by China in the United Nations, see Homer A. Jack, "Chinese Positions on Disarmament at the United Nations," in *Disarmament Report*, March 1, 1973, issued by SANE, the United Methodist Church, and the World Conference of Religion for Peace.

should give up underground testing so long as it feels a need to improve the size, yield, and reliability of its nuclear weapons through some form of testing. At the same time, Peking could decide that it is not in its interest to actively oppose the CTB, since the success of this agreement would help to preserve Peking's position as one of only five nuclear powers (or six, if India is included)—and, more specifically, would help to erect an additional barrier to the possibility of a nuclear Japan. Furthermore, taking a strongly negative position could involve significant political costs if Peking were to be accused of being irresponsible and blocking progress in the arms control field.

In sum, the likelihood of China's signing or supporting either the LTB or the CTB in the next few years is small. Probably the best that can be hoped for is that active Chinese opposition to them will diminish as the Chinese gain greater confidence in the deterrent capability of their growing nuclear force and become more aware of the advantages to China of halting nuclear proliferation.

Nuclear-Free Zones

Nuclear-free zones have been discussed in disarmament forums for many years, but thus far only the Latin American Denuclearization Treaty (Treaty of Tlatelolco) and the Antarctic Treaty have been negotiated, and there are no signs at present that accords in other regions will be negotiated within the next few years. The Chinese have signed Additional Protocol II of the Treaty of Tlatelolco, which is an undertaking by nuclear powers that they will respect the treaty and not use or threaten to use nuclear weapons against any of the contracting parties. (The treaty itself is for signature by Latin American states only.) This is the first post-1945 arms control convention that the Chinese have signed,[17] and thus constitutes an important step toward their cooperation with other nations in establishing significant, even though partial, controls on nuclear weapons.

The manner in which the Chinese were drawn, step by step, into agreeing to sign this protocol demonstrates how, as China becomes more active in international politics, it is likely to feel increasing pressure to accede to some arms control agreements or to join in negotiating future agreements. In December 1971, new to the United Nations and

17. The People's Republic of China is a party to one earlier arms control agreement, the Geneva Protocol of 1925 banning the use of bacteriological and chemical weapons. This convention was originally ratified by the Republic of China in 1929, and the PRC deposited its ratification in August 1952.

still feeling their way, the Chinese, while supporting in principle the concept of nuclear-free zones, declined to participate in the voting on a draft resolution urging nuclear powers to sign and ratify Additional Protocol II.[18] Less than a year later, in November 1972, the Chinese foreign minister, in a note to the Mexican ambassador in Peking, gave a series of specific assurances about how China would respect the nuclear-free character of the zone.[19] The Chinese declined at that time, however, to sign the protocol, on the technical ground that both protocol and treaty contained references to UN resolutions affirming the partial test ban treaty and the NPT, both of which China opposed. Finally, in April 1973, during a visit of the Mexican president to Peking, the Chinese announced that they intended to sign the protocol.[20] Perhaps one factor in their decision was that signing might improve China's image among developing countries relative to that of the USSR, which is now the only nuclear power not to have signed Additional Protocol II.

China has not signed the Antarctic Treaty, but if it saw political advantages in doing so it could sign without any significant adverse effect on its strategic position. Chinese adherence to this treaty would be valuable as a means of further involving the Chinese in multilateral arms control efforts, although the practical significance would be small.

The concept of NFZs has always been part of Peking's nuclear disarmament proposals. In the early 1960s, Chinese officials suggested establishing NFZs for all regions of the world as one of the steps toward complete nuclear disarmament. One Chinese proposal called for an NFZ in Asia and the Pacific region that would apply to the United States and the USSR as well as to China and would be tied to a mutual nonaggression pact. These particular proposals were never amplified and seemed designed largely for their propaganda effect, but they probably reflected a serious Chinese interest in the NFZ idea. Similarly, in early 1964, Chinese leaders expressed willingness to endorse a proposal for an African NFZ.

After China's first nuclear detonation, Peking maintained that no-first-use pledges must precede, or at least parallel, any steps to establish

18. Reported in FBIS, *Daily Report: People's Republic of China*, Dec. 3, 1971, p. A4.
19. Quoted in ibid., Nov. 15, 1972, pp. A17–A19.
20. Joint communiqué on the Echeverria visit; reported in ibid., April 24, 1973, pp. A1–A3.

NFZs. This position, first articulated in late 1964, was repeated in Chinese disarmament statements in 1971,[21] and it apparently continues to reflect China's insistence on its general policy that no-first-use pledges must form the foundation for meaningful nuclear arms control.[22] This policy is based on the argument that even the removal of weapons and the dismantling of bases in a region would not preclude the use of nuclear weapons against it from external launching points or through rapid redeployment of weapons. Thus, the nuclear powers must guarantee that they will not use nuclear weapons in particular nuclear-free zones in order to make NFZ agreements meaningful. In 1974, in voting for UNGA resolutions calling for the establishment of NFZs in South Asia and the Middle East, the Chinese spokesman declared that China was ready to undertake obligations not to use nuclear weapons against NFZs in these regions and called on other nuclear powers to do the same.[23]

Since China has continued to call for the withdrawal of nuclear weapons and means of delivery and the dismantling of overseas nuclear bases, it might be willing to give serious consideration to NFZs in Asian areas around its own borders. An NFZ accord relating to Northeast Asia—which might, for example, cover Korea and possibly later Japan—could help to reduce Peking's fears of a U.S. nuclear attack by removing the U.S. nuclear weapons that are now stationed close to China. Such an accord might also be politically significant to Peking as a sign of U.S. willingness to exercise nuclear restraint. Whether China would be prepared to forgo its insistence on prior no-first-use pledges in order to obtain such benefits, however, is unclear. It would be worth exploring whether China would in turn agree, if such an NFZ accord were reached, not to station its own nuclear weapons within a specified distance from its borders. The United States might under certain circumstances find a limited NFZ agreement to be consistent with its regional security interests and its arms control objectives in relation to China. Such an agreement might not be feasible, however, until China is capable of putting reconnaissance satellites into orbit so that its capacity to check

---

21. See speech by Chiao Kuan-hua at UNGA, Nov. 24, 1971; quoted in ibid., Nov. 29, 1971, p. A22.

22. See Chapter 5 for a discussion of the no-first-use issue.

23. Reported in FBIS, *Daily Report: People's Republic of China*, Nov. 25, 1974, pp. A2, A3.

on possible violations would be comparable to that of the other signatories to the agreement.[24]

Outer Space and Seabed Treaties

At present, China opposes the existing outer space and seabed
treaties,[25] but in some respects their attitude toward these treaties may
be less intense than toward the LTB and NPT, since they deal with
problems that are fairly remote from China's major concerns and have
fewer potential political implications for Chinese relations with Third
World countries.

Although there is no pressing need for China's accession to these
measures, it would be desirable to try to convince the Chinese that they
should participate in these as in other multilateral arms control treaties.
Since China has already launched a satellite, its adherence to the outer
space treaty would strengthen the long-term stability of the accord and
reduce fears that Peking might at some future date consider stationing
weapons of mass destruction in space. Likewise, the possibility of increased submarine development by China in the future argues for trying
to obtain Chinese adherence to the seabed treaty. In both cases, it is at
least possible that China may eventually come to see the benefits to be
derived from participating. However, China's nonparticipation has apparently not deterred other nations from supporting these measures and,
for at least the next decade, the basic effectiveness of these treaties will
not be impaired if China does not join.

Chemical and Biological Warfare Treaties

A treaty to ban biological warfare, destroy stocks of biological arms,
and prohibit laboratory experimentation with and development of such
arms was signed in 1972. China has criticized this agreement on the
grounds that it was a "sham disarmament" measure "cooked up" by the
two superpowers and, since it did not also ban chemical weapons, con-
stituted a step backward from the Geneva Protocol of 1925.[26] Nonetheless, it would be desirable to obtain China's participation in this agreement, and it is quite possible that Peking could see such an agreement

24. See Chapter 6 for a discussion of the possibility of an NFZ arrangement in
Korea.

25. See *Peking Review*, Feb. 10, 1967, p. 30, and March 5, 1971, p. 22.

26. See New China News Agency broadcast of Nov. 22, 1972; quoted in FBIS,
Daily Report: People's Republic of China, Nov. 24, 1972, p. A6.

as being in China's interest, since it would formalize restraints on the powers that have developed such weapons (not, as far as is known, including China). Indeed, some military analysts have pointed out that China's large size and population make it especially vulnerable to biological and chemical warfare. It should be noted that China has not only not shown any interest in developing weapons in this field, but it has ratified the Geneva Protocol.

A convention banning chemical warfare might well be concluded in the future. Many nations have been pressing for such a convention. Despite the many difficult problems of verification and control yet to be resolved, and even though the United States would find a pact banning chemical weapons somewhat more difficult to accept than a biological ban, such a pact is a real possibility and, under appropriate conditions, could be acceptable to the United States.

It is conceivable that Peking might be motivated to support a ban on chemical weapons by its relative disadvantage in producing such weapons, and it would be highly desirable to encourage such support. China's participation in negotiating even a single multilateral arms agreement of this type could begin to change its attitudes toward, and approach to, the entire field of international arms control. The fact that China did not itself participate in formulating past arms control agreements—and that the United States and the Soviet Union have been the prime initiators—may help to explain the negative Chinese attitude toward past agreements.

But now that China is seated in the United Nations, it is becoming involved in informal discussions of arms control. If the Chinese were offered the opportunity of participating in the processes of discussion, formulating, and negotiation that precede the formal agreement, the chances of obtaining Chinese support for it would be improved, and, what is perhaps more important, Peking might change its attitude toward future multilateral arms control agreements. This proposition can be tested by making serious efforts to involve China, where possible, in the early stages of consideration of certain proposals. A chemical warfare agreement could serve this purpose. Furthermore, arms control measures in the chemical and biological warfare spheres are not complicated by political problems and implications to the same extent as those in the nuclear field are. Broad international endorsement of such measures by Third World countries, as well as by others, would also help to induce China to consider participation.[27]

Conclusions

For the next few years, at least, China will probably refrain from participating in any of the major multilateral arms control agreements already signed. The possibility that the Chinese might join in negotiating future agreements during this period is somewhat greater, but still not large. China's failure to adhere to most of these agreements will not seriously damage their effectiveness. However, strong opposition by Peking to the NPT could reduce the prospects that certain countries will sign or ratify it. Moreover, continued hostility by Peking toward test bans and other limited nuclear arms control agreements could in the long run reduce international support for them.

In view of the relatively poor prospects of convincing the Chinese to participate in multilateral arms control, and the lack of urgent need to do so, it would be unwise and unnecessary for the United States to give this goal very high priority. Attempts to make China's participation a prerequisite to further multilateral agreements could, moreover, introduce unnecessary roadblocks to progress. Nonetheless, the United States should try to discuss the issues involved in multilateral arms control agreements in a bilateral U.S.–Chinese setting. China's eventual acquisition of a more reliable deterrent, and the gradual realization by Chinese leaders that arms control agreements could serve China's security interests by decreasing the risk of nuclear war and stabilizing the balance of forces in Asia, may in time lead Peking to reconsider its opposition to multilateral arms control measures.

Although the prospects of inducing the Chinese to sign or participate in negotiating multilateral arms control agreements during the next few years are not bright, the chances are better that they might lend tacit support to certain agreements—such as the NPT—that have clear benefits for Chinese interests. The Chinese could quietly support certain aspects of multilateral agreements without abandoning their public position of opposition to them as a scheme for perpetuating the nuclear dominance of the superpowers.

27. For a discussion of chemical and biological warfare issues and information on the Geneva Protocol, see *The Control of Chemical and Biological Weapons* (Carnegie Endowment, 1971).

CHAPTER FOUR

U.S. Arms Control Approaches toward China

Although the prospects for engaging China in multilateral arms control negotiations in the next few years are only fair, and though Chinese abstention from such negotiations would not—in the short term, at least—undermine existing agreements or prevent negotiations on new agreements from going ahead, it is in the interest of the United States to begin now to seek to engage China in a bilateral discussion of arms control.

Such a dialogue started now can accomplish a number of important purposes. Most important, it would serve to reduce the risk of nuclear war and might help slow down or prevent the proliferation of nuclear weapons. More generally, an arms control dialogue between the United States and China can serve as one element in an ongoing effort to improve relations between the two countries and to avoid a situation in which military deployments generate political tension and potential conflict.

Limited as China's military power and nuclear capabilities may now be, the development of a Chinese nuclear force poses some new problems for strategic stability. The very imbalance between U.S. and Chinese nuclear capabilities, and in particular the relative vulnerability of China's forces, might increase the risk of nuclear conflict. The mere existence of these forces raises the possibility of an unintentional nuclear exchange in a crisis situation. The complexities of the triangular United States–China–USSR relationship may also produce certain instabilities. It is therefore in the U.S. interest to try to minimize these dangers through arms control discussions and arrangements. Even if bilateral agreements cannot soon be reached, discussions could indirectly reduce risks by contributing to greater mutual understanding that could influence both nations' military policies and actions.

Arms control discussion between the United States and China can also help to increase the stability of Asia and avoid the likelihood of regional military clashes. Even though Peking is not likely to pursue high-risk military policies, the growth of China's nuclear power will inhibit to some extent U.S. freedom of action in responding to possible low-level military initiatives by the Chinese in Asia that run counter to U.S. regional security interests. If the Chinese could be drawn into regional arms control arrangements, the chances of U.S.–Chinese military conflict in Asia would be reduced, tensions between the two nations would be lessened, and the gradual mutual accommodation and normalization of relations now under way would be encouraged.

An arms control dialogue with China can also serve to make more effective the existing and potential worldwide arms control arrangements. The United States should attempt to develop an arms control strategy that will increase the likelihood of engaging China in meaningful discussions and might lead eventually to Chinese adherence to existing or new arms control arrangements. A more modest short-term aim should be to induce Peking to lend tacit support to these agreements or, at a minimum, not to oppose such measures actively. In the course of the next decade, it can be anticipated that the desirability of Chinese participation in arms control matters will steadily increase.

There might be disadvantages for the United States, of course, in engaging the Chinese in a dialogue on arms control, in terms of the reactions of other states, especially the USSR and Japan. In general, there is little reason to assume that a U.S.–Chinese dialogue would significantly damage U.S.–Soviet relations or diminish the prospects for Washington and Moscow reaching new arms control agreements. As for Japan, since virtually all Japanese favor measures that reduce the risk of war between the United States and China, it should not be difficult for the U.S. government to obtain official Japanese support for a U.S.–Chinese arms control dialogue if the Japanese government is consulted in advance and kept fully informed of the discussions.

The effort to engage China is sure to encounter many difficulties. The Chinese have not yet displayed any serious interest in arms control measures that might affect their own deployment of military forces; they have rather seen arms control largely in the context of what they view as an effort by the United States and the Soviet Union to come to limited agreements designed to establish bipolar hegemony over the world. They have also viewed specific arms control arrangements, particularly the limited test ban treaty, as aimed at constraining other nations and intended especially to prevent China from becoming a nuclear power. To date, China has opposed all U.S.–Soviet sponsored arms control agreements and has attempted to be the spokesman for the nonnuclear powers against the superpowers. At the same time, Peking has put forward sweeping nuclear disarmament proposals, which, by U.S. standards and in light of the history of actual arms control progress, appear to be unrealistic and propagandistic. Unless China adopts an approach to arms control that emphasizes the negotiation of limited measures designed to improve the stability of the strategic balance, little progress in negotiations is likely to be made.

Very little is known about internal Chinese debate on military matters. We do not know, for example, whether the Chinese have read and absorbed the arms control literature produced in the United States over the last decade. Strategic Arms Limitation Talks (SALT) negotiations have revealed that the Russians were more aware of these American analyses than had been supposed and that there were many Soviet officials who accepted them and were prepared to reason from the same premises. An arms control dialogue with China would reveal whether there are Chinese counterparts to the Soviet and American technicians who have carried out much of the negotiations at SALT; if the Chinese do not now have such expertise, the dialogue would help to create it.

Present Chinese attitudes toward arms control can be explained in a number of ways. The Chinese may be reluctant to engage in talks with the United States or the USSR because, as champions of the developing nations, they have frequently declared that China would never be a superpower; to engage in talks on nuclear matters with a superpower might appear to undermine this stance. China's relative military weakness probably makes its leaders wary about engaging in serious arms control negotiations because they genuinely believe that any limited arms control arrangement backed by the superpowers must aim at keeping China permanently in an inferior position. Given the wide gap between the nuclear capabilities of the superpowers and China, the Chinese may believe that for some time to come China can gain more from exploiting the disarmament issue for political and propagandistic purposes than from entering into serious negotiations. Finally, Chinese leaders may oppose certain arms control measures simply because they do not appreciate the fact that limited, cooperative arrangements could enhance China's security.

There are reasons to believe, however, that the Chinese might become more receptive to arms control over the next several years. It is clear that Peking's leaders are intensely concerned about China's national security problems; in particular, they now fear Soviet intentions and are apprehensive about the possibility of major Japanese remilitarization. Perhaps Peking will gradually come to realize that arms control measures can decrease the risk of nuclear war and proliferation, reduce the danger of conflict with both the United States and the USSR, and contribute to regional stability in Asia in ways that can serve China's long-term security interests. It is reasonable to believe, also, that the political leaders of China are concerned about the diversion of resources from economic to military purposes and that some leaders have argued for the need to reduce military spending. The Chinese thus may come to see arms control as providing a way to limit their military budget and to forgo some costly military expenditures. Moreover, the Chinese leaders who are committed to an effort to improve relations with the United States may see limited arms control measures as one area in which progress may be possible that will serve to improve the overall relationship.

Even though the short-run prospects for meaningful discussions with China are not bright, the effort to initiate them should be begun now, since it is likely to take a long time from the beginning of such arms control discussions to the negotiation of important agreements. Bilateral U.S.–Chinese discussions should not be regarded as a substitute for Chinese participation in multilateral forums; on the contrary, an important purpose of bilateral talks would be to encourage China eventually to join in serious multilateral negotiations. But most of the issues worth exploring with China at this stage are probably better discussed in an American-Chinese forum, official or non-official. Even arms control arrangements that would require the participation of the other powers, such as those concerning Korea or other regions, can best be discussed initially in bilateral talks conducted by the United States with China and the other powers concerned.

In considering the possible results from opening an arms control dialogue between the United States and China, more emphasis should be placed on developing tacit understandings, particularly in the early years, than on reaching explicit agreements. As the Chinese become more active generally on the international scene, they are developing an increasingly sophisticated perception of where China's interests lie. The tolerance toward the U.S.–Japanese security treaty and the presence of U.S. forces in East Asia expressed privately by Chinese officials during 1973 and 1974 is a good example of their growing willingness to make tactical compromises that are quite in contrast to their official statements. Similarly, as the Chinese study the evolving attitudes of other nations toward arms control, they may discover a number of areas in which Chinese interests parallel those of the United States and thus be able to reach tacit agreements with the United States on positions or lines of action, even where they would reject explicit agreements.

Four Arms Control Packages

A consideration of the specific issues that should be discussed in arms control talks with the Chinese should be preceded by a definition of objectives. Four objectives of potential interest to China as well as the United States can be identified: (1) to reduce the possibility of accidental or unauthorized nuclear launches and other accidents; (2) to reduce the tension in U.S.–Chinese relations arising from Chinese fear of a U.S. nuclear first strike; (3) to reduce sources of instability in Asia by putting arms control in the context of regional military and political agreements; (4) to enhance the effectiveness of multilateral arms control agreements by obtaining Chinese adherence or informal support.

To accomplish these objectives, the United States should consider adopting certain linked sets of actions, or "packages," to include topics for discussion, bilateral arrangements, and unilateral U.S. actions that are mutually consistent and reinforcing.

Package One: Technical Measures

The objective of this package is to reduce the possibility of accidental or unauthorized launching of nuclear weapons or of other accidental events leading to nuclear war. A single nuclear explosion or firing of a nuclear missile, particularly in a crisis situation, could lead to all-out nuclear war; and, while accidental or unauthorized launches could occur at any time, the risk is greatest during periods of heightened political tension.

When political leaders see tensions mounting and the danger of war growing, they are likely to ready their forces for nuclear war; this is especially likely if their nuclear defense relies heavily on early-generation ICBMs of the kind that the Russians had through the 1960s and the Chinese are now developing. The steps that must be taken to put weapons on alert for immediate firing increase the danger of nuclear accidents. Moreover, in a crisis there is always the danger that a local military commander with the authority to fire nuclear weapons might decide to do so in the mistaken belief that nuclear war is imminent. One also cannot rule out the risk that a local military commander might decide that nuclear war is necessary or inevitable and seek to trigger it by firing the weapons at his command. Even though the probability of accidental or unauthorized use may be very low in China, all these reasons make it desirable to initiate a discussion with Peking about the problems of accidental or unauthorized launching.

There are several unilateral steps that the United States could take to facilitate this process. The United States has already gone far in designing a strategic force that does not depend on launch-on-warning for survivability. The United States should avoid taking any steps in the future that would make its strategic forces more vulnerable to Chinese weapons and hence need to be put on alert in a nuclear crisis. If, for example, the United States were to rely on bombers stationed within range of Chinese medium-range ballistic missiles (MRBMs) for part of its deterrent against China, it might feel it necessary to put such forces on airborne alert in a crisis. Such an alert could in turn increase Chinese fears of American attack—fears that would be especially acute until China's forces are less vulnerable than they are now—thus increasing the danger of preemptive or accidental launching. The United States can also contribute to the stability of the strategic balance in a crisis situation by refraining from initiating provocative intelligence-gathering operations such as aircraft overflights of the Chinese mainland. Overflights during a crisis could trigger Chinese fears that they were designed to gather last-minute intelligence for an attack and again increase the danger of accidental or unauthorized launches.

The dialogue on the question of reducing the likelihood of accidental or unauthorized use might begin with a unilateral presentation of the American understanding of this problem and an offer to provide China with whatever technical information it can about the command and control procedures currently used by the United States. Such a transfer of information should be as technical as possible, within the constraints imposed by the need to maintain the security of some American systems and procedures. Within these limits it should be possible to give the Chinese a substantial amount of information that could affect their policies and behavior, whether or not they reciprocated with comparable information of their own.

One of our major purposes should be to convey to China information and technology that it could use to improve control of its strategic forces —an objective that is especially important because of China's relatively vulnerable systems. Another goal should be to reassure the Chinese that American weapons will not be fired accidentally or on an unauthorized basis against China. Offering China information on our systems could produce substantial political gains in terms of reassuring China without any significant costs to the United States. In order to avoid some of the problems inherent in discussing delicate strategic issues, however, the United States would have to be careful not to imply that it believes Peking is irresponsible in its handling of nuclear weapons and not to overstate the present vulnerability of Chinese forces.

The transfer of command and control information would provide a context for the discussion of the problem of unauthorized or accidental use of nuclear weapons. American negotiators could convey to their Chinese colleagues their understanding of the problem and seek to learn how China sees the problem and what it plans to do to reduce the dangers involved, particularly given the soft and cumbersome nature of China's first-generation systems.

If these discussions should elicit any interest on the part of Peking in discussing specific bilateral measures to reduce the risk of accidental or unauthorized use, the United States could propose three agreements similar to those already concluded with the Soviet Union as collateral measures at the Strategic Arms Limitation Talks: an agreement on a hot line, an agreement to prevent accidental launching of nuclear weapons, and an agreement on the prevention of nuclear war.

A Washington-Peking hot line, which now appears feasible because of the "liaison offices" in both capitals, could be important symbolically, as well as in permitting rapid communication during crises so as to minimize possible escalation to the point of conflict. An agreement to consult in the event of accidental nuclear detonation, requiring action by both sides to prevent accidents as well as to consult in order to prevent conflict if accidents do occur, should help to reduce existing risks. And an agreement to "exclude" nuclear war and to initiate "urgent consultations" when there appears to be any risk of nuclear conflict should help to stabilize both bilateral and multilateral strategic relations.

It is impossible now to judge when, or even if, Peking might be prepared to discuss such agreements, but continuing efforts should be made to ascertain Chinese views on these subjects.

Package Two: Tension-Reducing Measures

If, as argued in Chapter 1, there is little risk that during the next few years the Chinese might launch a major attack with conventional forces on a neighboring territory, the United States should give serious consideration to measures that would reduce the tensions in the U.S.–Chinese relationship that arise out of Chinese fear of an American nuclear first strike. A number of steps toward this end are worth considering.

Although Peking probably now views Moscow as posing the greatest potential military threat in the short run, the Chinese have on a number of occasions since 1949 feared an American nuclear attack. Before their intervention in the Korean war, Chinese leaders debated whether such action would lead to the use of atomic weapons by the United States. Even after they intervened, the Chinese still apparently believed that there was a significant possibility that America would attack China. In 1953, President Eisenhower explicitly warned Peking that the United States might use nuclear weapons against the Chinese mainland if the Korean war was not promptly brought to an end. During the 1954–55 and 1958 offshore islands crises, the United States again explicitly or implicitly threatened the possible use of nuclear weapons, and, according to President Eisenhower,[1] Washington was in fact ready to use nuclear weapons if either crisis had significantly escalated. There have been unconfirmed published reports that the Kennedy administration at one time considered attempting to destroy embryonic Chinese nuclear capacity, and the Chinese might well have feared that a nuclear strike for such a purpose was indeed possible.[2]

President Nixon's trip to Peking and the actions that the United States has taken both before and since have probably gone a long way toward reducing Chinese fear of American nuclear attack. The U.S. government no longer takes the view that it held in the 1950s that the over-

1. Dwight D. Eisenhower, *The White House Years*, vol. 1, *Mandate for Change, 1953–1956* (Doubleday, 1963), p. 477.
2. Ralph E. Lapp, *The Weapons Culture* (Norton, 1968), pp. 74–75.

throw of the communist regime in China and the restoration of Nationalist rule on the mainland is a serious possibility. The United States indicates by its actions as well as its words that it now accepts the People's Republic of China as the government of the Chinese mainland. Nevertheless, efforts to reduce tension and hostility between the two countries would probably be facilitated by a conscious American attempt to allay still further Chinese fears of a possible nuclear attack. In addition to the steps that have already been discussed, a number of others are possible. The U.S. decision to forgo building a Chinese-oriented ABM system should help to persuade the Chinese that the United States is not seeking a first-strike capability. To reinforce this perception in China, the United States should also forgo deployment of weapons systems whose major purpose would be to enhance the ability of the United States to limit or deny China the capability of inflicting damage on U.S. targets. Such a damage limitation policy might well be viewed by Peking as one designed to achieve a first-strike capability.

The United States should also seek an opportunity to explain to Peking its concept of deterrence, emphasizing its view that the value of nuclear weapons is primarily, if not entirely, to deter nuclear attacks by other countries. At the same time, the United States should try to elicit Chinese views of deterrence and learn what in the American nuclear posture may appear threatening to Peking. We can learn from the case of the Soviet Union, where U.S. military planners probably did not pay sufficient attention to the Soviet concerns about American tactical nuclear forces in Europe that are capable of reaching the Soviet Union. It may also be that our perceptions of what concerns the Chinese are inaccurate and that frank discussions could reveal what aspects of the U.S. military posture the Chinese find most disturbing.

Such discussions would not be without difficulties and risks. A full explanation by the United States of its concept of what constitutes a stable and secure deterrent force could sound patronizing to the Chinese, implying that China not only lacks such a capability now but is unlikely to have it in the foreseeable future. A U.S. statement that nuclear weapons have the *primary* function of deterring nuclear attack might be interpreted as an implicit threat that under certain circumstances the United States might consider initiating the use of nuclear weapons against China. It would be important to avoid conveying the impression that the United States might consider first use of nuclear weapons against China in a crisis generated by others, with the purpose of trying to force Peking to cease giving aid to its allies.

In the past, American military deployments in East Asia and overflights, or alleged overflights, of Chinese territory have been a source of tension between the United States and China. The Chinese have issued a number of "serious warnings" about American intrusions on Chinese air and sea space, many of which appear to indicate that the two countries have different notions about where Chinese territory ends. No such warnings have been given since President Nixon's visit to China, suggesting that the improved political climate has either caused the Chinese to drop the practice of issuing "serious warnings" or caused the United States to avoid routing planes and ships near such sensitive areas as the Paracel Islands in the South China Sea—probably both explanations are valid. Now that continuous channels of official communication exist between Washington and Peking, the United States can make use of them to explain the actions of U.S. naval vessels and aircraft whenever it is necessary for them to pass through areas where their presence might seem provocative to the Chinese.

Chinese fear of an American nuclear attack could be substantially reduced if the United States were prepared to propose to Peking some sort of no-first-use pledge or agreement. Such a pledge would make it possible for the United States to present its views of the strategic balance in ways that did not appear threatening to Peking. A worldwide, unqualified no-first-use pledge, such as the Chinese have demanded of all nuclear powers, would create problems for the United States in parts of the world that are beyond the scope of this study. The Chinese have not, however, expressly ruled out other forms of no-first-use pledges and have even indicated that such a pledge might take the form of an agreement.

A no-first-use pledge toward China should be seriously considered by the United States for a number of reasons. It would strengthen a desirable tendency to think increasingly of nuclear weapons as usable only to deter their use by others, not as suitable for responding to conventional attacks, and would therefore tend to diminish the importance of nuclear weapons in the eyes of others, thus discouraging proliferation. Moreover, given the great emphasis the Chinese have placed on no-first-use pledges by nuclear powers as an essential first step toward other forms of arms control, a U.S. pledge might open the door to other arms control agreements. Only by trying to engage the Chinese in discussion of this subject can it be determined whether Peking's position on no first use is adopted for propaganda purposes or is flexible enough to offer an opening for wider-ranging arms control negotiations. Finally, serious consideration of a no-first-use pledge toward China would force a critical examination of the contingencies in which the United States might in theory consider the first use of nuclear weapons against China, including the realistic evaluation of the chances of such contingencies arising and the potential costs to the United States of first use.[3]

Package Three: Regional Stability Measures

Another approach to arms control discussions with China would aim at concluding agreements that, in connection with other political and diplomatic moves, would help to reduce tensions and increase stability in certain areas of potential conflict in Asia.

Separate arms control measures could be designed to apply specifically to several different regions around China's borders. One possible region is Southeast Asia. Consideration could be given to methods of creating a "zone of peace, freedom, and neutrality" there, as proposed by the foreign ministers of the Association of Southeast Asian Nations in 1971, to limiting the outside supply of weapons or the presence of foreign military bases or troops, and to concluding agreements forbidding or limiting big-power military intervention in the area. The form and specific content of such agreements would depend greatly on future developments resulting from the North Vietnamese victory over South Vietnam; no attempt is made here to examine the various possibilities.

A second region where arms control might help to reduce political tensions is the Taiwan Strait. President Nixon committed the United States in the Shanghai communiqué to "progressively reduce its forces and military installations on Taiwan as the tension in the area diminishes," with the "ultimate objective" of total withdrawal. Concrete steps in this direction would be desirable in the period ahead, while maintaining, under existing circumstances, our insistence that any resolution of the Taiwan problem be peaceful. This would demonstrate to Peking that the United States does not intend to use Taiwan for American military bases directed at China and is willing to accept future changes in Taiwan's status so long as they are peacefully accomplished. To the extent that relations between the United States and China continue to improve, the U.S. concern with the defense of Taiwan will tend to

3. See Chapter 5 for a detailed discussion of no-first-use pledges.

decline in importance—a process that is already under way as a result of the Shanghai communiqué.

Reduction in size of the American military presence—totaling fewer than 5,000 persons as of 1975—or its complete withdrawal from Taiwan would not significantly weaken the Chinese Nationalists' security position or the capacity of the United States to deter a military attack on the island. Nor is there any reason to believe that it would encourage Peking to consider an "adventuristic" military attack there. All available evidence points to the conclusion that Peking views the problem in long-range political terms, and, moreover, that it lacks the naval, amphibious, and other capabilities necessary seriously to threaten Taiwan. The Chinese Nationalists possess a strong defense force, and the U.S. Seventh Fleet is adequate under existing conditions to deter and, if present trends in U.S.–Chinese relations were reversed, to defend against amphibious attack.

In the past the Chinese have proposed the creation of nuclear-free zones in the Asian area. These proposals raise a number of questions, including whether such zones would include a portion of China. Problems of inspection are difficult ones, as are those created by the fact that nuclear weapons can be flown into an area very quickly. Discussion of this issue is hindered by the fact that the United States does not reveal where it keeps nuclear weapons outside its own territory.

However, the United States could consider entering into an agreement to make the Taiwan Strait area a nuclear-free zone, or it could consider taking unilateral action aimed, explicitly or tacitly, at this goal. Consideration might also be given to the possibility of agreeing that within a larger area—to include some part of the Chinese mainland as well as Taiwan and the islands in the Taiwan Strait—both sides would agree not to store or to use nuclear weapons, without reference to what the political future of the area might be. The feasibility of such approaches to arms control in the area will depend on the evolution of the overall political relations between the United States and China and on the way in which the Taiwan issue evolves in that context.

The most likely area for the establishment of arms control measures, linked to other stabilizing agreements, in the period immediately ahead would seem to be Korea. A set of interlocking agreements relating to Korea would need to involve six nations, including South and North Korea and the four major powers with strong interests in the area—the United States, Japan, China, and the Soviet Union. The obligations to be undertaken by the United States and China would include commitments to maintain Korea as a nuclear-free zone and to refrain from the use of force on the Korean peninsula.[4]

The potentialities for conflict involving the major powers that could threaten the security of Asia as a whole are particularly great in Korea. Not only do the two heavily armed Korean regimes face each other with intense hostility, but each of the four major powers believes that it has important security interests at stake there. Each fears domination of the Korean peninsula by any one of the others, and any conflict there could rapidly involve all four. To a certain extent all four major powers probably recognize this fact, although in differing ways and degrees, and this common perception of danger could provide the basis for discussions among them about how to reduce the risks of a major conflict.

Package Four: Existing Arms Control Arrangements

Another major goal of U.S. policy should be to involve China, ultimately, in existing and future worldwide arms control arrangements. The obstacles to achieving this objective were discussed in Chapter 3, with the conclusion that, although prospects for immediate success are not bright, the United States should try to engage the Chinese in bilateral discussions on arms control matters. This would have the double goal of broadening the area of common understanding between the two nations and making it more likely that China will expressly or tacitly support existing arms control agreements (or at least not actively oppose them) and eventually take part in the negotiation of new agreements.

Proposing to the Chinese a formal discussion of the advantages to be gained from joining multilateral arms control arrangements or negotiations is unlikely to be productive. Even if the Chinese were to agree to meet with the United States for this purpose, the discussion could easily harden present Chinese positions, given their suspicion of all arms control activities initiated by the superpowers. But a low-key presentation of U.S. views on arms control, introduced discreetly into the discussion of related subjects or into general exchanges of views on world affairs, might gradually bring the Chinese to see the advantages to China as well as to other nations of a step-by-step approach to the ultimate goal of general and complete disarmament, including the elimination of nuclear weapons. In short, informal discussion of this topic would probably be more effective than formal exchanges.

4. See Chapter 6.

But the topics for a U.S.–Chinese dialogue on multilateral arms control measures must be carefully chosen. U.S. efforts to persuade the Chinese to support the limited test ban (LTB) or comprehensive test ban (CTB), for example, would probably be counterproductive. Given the great U.S. superiority over China in nuclear weapons, for the United States to urge China to halt nuclear testing can only seem self-serving to the Chinese. Efforts to enlist Chinese support for these measures are best left to nonnuclear powers.

The nonproliferation treaty (NPT) is a more likely topic for a U.S.–Chinese dialogue, since both countries share an interest in preventing nuclear proliferation. A candid and continuing exchange of views on this subject, reinforced by representations to China by nonnuclear supporters of the NPT, would encourage the Chinese to give at least tacit support to the treaty and perhaps eventually to adopt a position similar to that of France—that is, a public announcement that it would act as if it had signed the treaty and would assume all the obligations placed by it on nuclear powers.

While discussion with the Chinese of the outer space and seabed treaties probably would not significantly increase the likelihood of early Chinese adherence to them, it would provide an opportunity for Americans and Chinese to gain a clearer understanding of the value each places on such partial arms control measures. The same is true of the biological warfare treaty and the proposed treaty on chemical weapons. The more the Chinese can be drawn into detailed discussion with the United States and other nations of concrete partial arms control measures, the more likely it is that they will come to recognize the advantages that some of these measures hold for China and that their continued adamant opposition to such measures will entail significant political costs.

Forums

The United States could seek to initiate an arms control dialogue with China in a variety of ways. Official talks would obviously be necessary in order to reach agreement between the two governments, but it might prove easier to sound out the Chinese on some subjects through unofficial channels.

Bilateral Official U.S.–China Talks

Washington should be prepared to discuss strategic and arms control issues with Peking through any of several bilateral channels, including the liaison offices in Peking and Washington, the United Nations missions of both nations in New York, visits to Peking by high-level U.S. representatives, and special official meetings convened specifically to discuss such issues.

Both countries raised some arms control issues at the Warsaw discussions, but the dialogue was rather formal, the political context was unfavorable, and the measures put forward by both were one-sided and sometimes seemed almost to be designed to be nonnegotiable. Bilateral discussions in the improved atmosphere created by steps toward normalization of relations might prove to be more productive. Following the pattern of the bilateral U.S.–Soviet SALT negotiations, discussions between the United States and China could be held with maximum privacy and might include informal as well as formal sessions.

SALT

For the reasons explored in Chapter 3, it seems neither feasible nor desirable for China to be invited to participate at present in the U.S.–Soviet SALT negotiations. At some future time, however, especially after China has acquired a reliable deterrent, a mechanism might be found for involving Peking—along with Britain and France—in these strategic arms limitations discussions.

Other Forums

Some of the proposals made in this study, such as the proposed set of agreements relating to Korea, would require at some stage special conferences or forums of the parties directly concerned. These would have to be explored in connection with the specific proposals.

Unofficial Discussions

All the above suggestions concern possible official approaches aimed at initiating an intergovernmental dialogue with the Chinese. One other possibility also deserves mention—namely, an attempt to initiate unofficial discussions of strategic and arms control issues, in meetings of a "Pugwash" type. Unofficial discussions of this sort could either precede or parallel efforts made on an official level. Many believe that the Pugwash meetings in the 1960s helped to create a basis for common discourse by U.S. and Soviet arms control specialists and thereby paved the way for SALT. It would be desirable for private initiatives to be made from time to time by one or more major private American academic or research institutions or by an ad hoc group of qualified scholars. Exactly how feelers might best be extended, or to whom, cannot be defined in advance; it might depend entirely on unpredictable opportunities that could arise. How the Chinese might respond to proposals for unofficial meetings is just as uncertain, of course, as the degree of their responsiveness to official initiatives. But even though initial Chinese reactions might be discouraging, the possibility of changes in their viewpoint over time argues for a continued pursuit of dialogue through a variety of approaches.

Tactics and Timing

The four packages put forward above are in no sense mutually exclusive. The proposed Korean arms control agreements constitute the package that is in some respects the most clearly separable from the others. The United States should thus begin discussions with its allies, Japan and South Korea, about the feasibility of possible forms of international arrangements regarding Korea and then try to initiate informal discussions about them with Peking and Moscow. The Chinese are likely, at least at the start, to view such discussions mainly in political and diplomatic terms, rather than in an arms control context, so that their response is likely to be shaped largely by their perception of the political and diplomatic repercussions.

In regard to the other three packages, in any dialogue between the United States and China, whether in a special forum or in other ongoing negotiating channels, the United States will have to choose from the start which goals to emphasize. While it would be possible to introduce elements from each of the three packages in the early stages of any negotiations, it would probably be preferable for the United States to establish its priorities in advance and to begin the dialogue slowly, focusing at first on a few—perhaps one or two—key issues.

Which goals the United States decides to pursue initially will depend in part on what position it concludes it can adopt on specific arms control measures, particularly on the question of no first use. If the United

States concludes that it cannot offer to negotiate any form of no-first-use arrangement with Peking, then it probably should begin the discussions with issues relating to technical measures, perhaps proceeding thereafter to discussion of existing arms control agreements. It, on the other hand, the United States is prepared to discuss some kind of no-first-use pledge with Peking, it should introduce that subject at once, both because Peking seems most interested in it and because it could open the way to discussion of other arms control issues.

Whatever the choice, it is important to begin to talk with Peking about arms control in the near future. Arms control has played a major role in the alleviation of tension between the United States and the Soviet Union, and it is conceivable—and certainly to be hoped—that it could play a comparable role in U.S.–Chinese relations in the years ahead.

Implications for U.S. Relations with the USSR and Japan

A dialogue between the United States and China on arms control—and any agreements that resulted—could have significant repercussions on U.S. relations with the Soviet Union and Japan. Maintaining the strategic balance with the USSR, and ensuring that Japan does not feel compelled to rearm massively or to go nuclear, are both of vital importance to the security of the United States. U.S. economic interests in Japan and Japanese cooperation in shaping the international economic order are also of great importance to Americans. Consequently, the United States must try to minimize any adverse effects on its relations with the USSR and Japan that its arms control explorations with China might have.

The Soviet Union can be expected to be suspicious of U.S. efforts to reach arms control agreements with China. It is highly improbable, however, that this would cause the USSR to refuse to work seriously toward follow-up SALT agreements or to take a negative stance on other multilateral arms control measures such as the CTB. The Russians have a large stake in the relationship they have now established with the United States, especially in the field of arms control, which they would be reluctant to jeopardize.

Moreover, it can be argued with considerable justification that a U.S.–Chinese dialogue on arms control might have a favorable rather than an unfavorable effect on future U.S.–Soviet negotiations on arms control and other matters. Certainly, President Nixon's visit to Peking appears to have had a favorable effect in this regard on his subsequent visit to Moscow. Since both China and the Soviet Union now seem seriously interested in improving relations with the United States and concerned lest the other get ahead in this respect, an arms control dialogue with China might have the effect of encouraging Moscow to seek further improvement in its relations with Washington.

The Russians should, of course, recognize that a positive Chinese attitude toward arms control would have advantages for them, also— for many of the same reasons that it will for the United States. The USSR supports nonproliferation, for example, and must realize that Chinese opposition to the NPT and refusal to stop nuclear testing could, in time, increase the risk of proliferation. On the strategic level, the USSR obviously shares the U.S. interest in ensuring that China's growing nuclear capability does not endanger U.S.–Soviet stability or block further progress in the SALT negotiations. The Russians also share the United States' concern about accidental nuclear war. Leonid Brezhnev, in a speech to the Trade Union Congress in March 1972, spoke approvingly of the U.S.–Soviet Nuclear Accidents Agreement and added that "the Soviet Union comes out for other nuclear powers to participate in such an arrangement in some form."[5]

The United States, in addition to avoiding actions that might damage U.S.–Soviet relations, should try to persuade the USSR of the advantages of U.S.–Chinese arms control discussions. The risk of negative Soviet reactions might be minimized if the United States were to begin its discussions with China by raising the technical matters described in package one. The United States should also explain to the USSR—perhaps in the context of the later stages of SALT—the purpose of its approach to the Chinese, highlighting in particular such goals as reducing the risk of accidental nuclear war and halting proliferation. Another possible benefit of U.S. arms control discussions with China is that any positive results might, in some instances, enhance the chances for useful discussions on the same topic between Moscow and Peking. For example, Chinese agreement to a Washington-Peking hot line might encourage a similar arrangement eventually between Moscow and Peking.

The Japanese will also be very sensitive to arms control negotiations between the United States and China. They are already ambivalent

5. Quoted in Foreign Broadcast Information Service, *Daily Report: Soviet Union,* March 21, 1972, p. J-16.

about U.S. relations with China: on the one hand, they would doubtless welcome the decreased tension and diminished risk of war that would result from arms control agreements between Peking and Washington; but, on the other hand, they might fear that these agreements and the improved relations between the United States and China would work to Japan's disadvantage. Some Japanese fear that the reduction of U.S. forces in the western Pacific under the Nixon doctrine may be intended to shift the security burden in that region to Japan, which would increase the possibility of a future confrontation between Japan and China. Other Japanese fear the opposite—that the United States may be colluding with China to keep Japan militarily weak. Still others take the improvement of U.S. relations with China to mean that Japan can no longer rely to the same extent on the U.S. defense commitment to it. These are all minority views in Japan, which so far have not seriously threatened the determination of Liberal Democratic Party leaders to rely on the U.S.–Japan security treaty and keep Japan a lightly armed, nonnuclear power; but it would not be in the U.S. interest to take actions that reinforced such minority views.

The existence of these Japanese reactions does not argue against a U.S. approach to China on arms control, but makes it clear that great care must be taken if serious damage to U.S.–Japanese relations is to be avoided. The Japanese government must be approached in advance and persuaded that the U.S. dialogue with China is in the best interests of both the United States and Japan. The Japanese must also be consulted in good faith as the negotiations proceed. Japanese suspicion of secret negotiations between the United States and China, and Chinese suspicion that the United States might conspire to remilitarize Japan, create a very delicate problem. Allaying suspicions on both sides requires that negotiations be kept as much as possible in the public view, without allowing them to deteriorate into a propaganda exercise. The Japanese, like the Soviets, would probably find it easier to understand and accept a U.S.–Chinese discussion of technical matters, such as ways to prevent accidental firings, than of subjects with broader political implications, such as no-first-use pledges or nuclear-free zones.

Conclusions

Although it is less urgent and important for the United States to engage China in arms control negotiations than to engage the USSR,

Chinese abstention from such negotiations will be increasingly damaging to U.S. interests as the years go by and the Chinese nuclear force grows. A U.S.–Chinese dialogue could reduce the danger of an accidental or unauthorized launching of nuclear missiles and could diminish the tension arising from Chinese vulnerability to a U.S. first strike. It could also lead to agreements to improve regional stability and might help persuade Peking to adhere to, or at least give tacit support to, certain existing multilateral arms control agreements or ongoing negotiations.

No dramatic results are likely soon. It may be several years before Peking will see the advantages in serious discussion of arms control with the United States. Nonofficial talks are perhaps a more feasible starting point than official discussions. But for the very reason that concrete results of a dialogue on arms control are likely to be slow in appearing, the United States should give serious thought now to ways of getting that dialogue started.

CHAPTER FIVE

A U.S. No-First-Use Pledge

There are a number of reasons why the United States should give serious consideration to the possibility of pledging that it would not use nuclear weapons first against China. At first glance, the advantages of such a no-first-use (NFU) pledge do not seem compelling and its disadvantages loom large. Because of the great disparity in nuclear capability between the two nations, the United States would appear to gain little by such action, while China would receive important advantages without giving anything in return, since it has already made an unqualified pledge never to use nuclear weapons first. Yet closer examination of the proposition makes its advantages more apparent and its drawbacks less troubling

Types of NFU Pledges

An NFU pledge is a declaration that a nation will not be the first to use nuclear weapons. A nuclear power theoretically could declare that it would *never* use nuclear weapons—that is, deny itself the option of nuclear retaliation even if nuclear weapons were used against it. In practice, however, such retaliation could never be ruled out. Thus, it is doubtful that nonuse pledges between nuclear powers would be credible, except in the context of a universal ban on producing and stockpiling nuclear weapons. In the present world situation, nuclear no-first-use pledges are more feasible than nonuse pledges between nuclear powers, since a nation making an NFU pledge retains the capacity and right to retaliate against nuclear attack, which serves as a deterrent against first strikes by others.

A pledge by a nuclear power never to use nuclear weapons against a nonnuclear power, on the other hand, would be feasible and credible. Since none of the present nuclear powers faces a military threat from a nonnuclear state that could not easily be met with its conventional weapons, a nonuse pledge of this type by a nuclear power would involve no increased security risks for it. Those nuclear powers, including the United States and China, that have signed Additional Protocol II of the Latin American Denuclearization Treaty have, in fact, made such nonuse pledges toward the signatories of that treaty.

A no-first-use pledge could take various forms. It could be unilateral, negotiated and announced jointly by two powers, or agreed to multilaterally by several nations. Peking has urged that the United States and the USSR agree to make unilateral NFU pledges, applicable worldwide. However, the possible effects of a worldwide NFU pledge on relations with our European allies and on U.S.–Soviet relations raise complex questions that are beyond the scope of this analysis; this discussion is restricted to a consideration of various options relating specifically to the United States and China, or to specified Asian areas, in the framework of an overall U.S. arms control approach toward China.[1]

A joint U.S.–Chinese NFU pledge could be made applicable to any use of nuclear force against the territory or forces of either nation. The political implications of a joint pledge—that the two countries share a common concern about nuclear problems—would have somewhat different effects from parallel unilateral American and Chinese pledges. Such an agreement might also provide that any use of nuclear weapons in Asia by either party would release the other from its pledge. This provision would ensure against the Chinese use, or threat of use, of nuclear weapons against our allies or any other Asian nation considered vital to U.S. interests. Another possibility would be a unilateral U.S. pledge restricted to Chinese territory and Chinese forces; this, in effect, would parallel, though in more restricted terms, the NFU pledge China has already made. It could, however, be made conditional on China's maintaining its NFU pledge, thus effectively making the two pledges reciprocal even without any new action by China. Still a third possibility, which could be combined with either of the foregoing options, would be NFU pledges applied to specified regions. Such accords could be made

1. For a thoughtful discussion of the potential advantages and disadvantages to the United States of a U.S. global NFU pledge, see Richard Ullman, "No First Use of Nuclear Weapons," *Foreign Affairs*, vol. 50 (July 1972), pp. 669–83.

conditional upon other political or military agreements. For example, bilateral or regional NFU pledges could be linked to a mutual renunciation of the use of force and the establishment of a nuclear-free zone in Korea,[2] and they could also involve other nations.

There are other actions that the United States could take unilaterally that would produce some of the benefits of a U.S. NFU pledge while avoiding the undesirable impact on U.S. allies that such a pledge might have. These could include reaching a consensus within the U.S. government that first use of nuclear weapons against China was a most unlikely contingency and revamping U.S. military planning and the deployment of nuclear weapons—especially tactical nuclear weapons—accordingly, with an explanation to the Chinese of why the United States was taking such actions. Although this policy would probably be less effective in drawing the Chinese into arms control negotiations than an NFU pledge, it would help to diminish Chinese fears of a possible U.S. first strike against China and would not have the potential for complicating relations with our allies that an NFU pledge would. Of course, our principal allies, especially Japan, would have to be informed in confidence of this policy, but the repercussions would be much less severe.

Still another possibility is a U.S. pledge not to use nuclear weapons against nonnuclear states. The Chinese, in urging the United States and the USSR to make NFU pledges, have placed special emphasis on this point.[3] The United States could respond to Peking by proposing a bilateral agreement—either general or limited to Asia—on refraining from the use of nuclear weapons against nonnuclear states. Washington and Peking could also call on other nuclear powers to join in such a declaration.

Chinese Interest in No First Use

The no-first-use idea has for some years been central, indeed crucial, element in China's public arms control policy. After its initial nuclear detonation in 1964, the Chinese government unilaterally declared that "at no time and in no circumstances will China be the first to use

2. See Chapter 6.

3. See speech by Chinese Vice Foreign Minister Chiao Kuan-hua to the UN General Assembly, Oct. 3, 1972; reported in Foreign Broadcast Information Service (FBIS), *Daily Report: People's Republic of China*, Oct. 6, 1972, p. A10.

nuclear weapons." It called for all present and potential nuclear powers
to agree not to use nuclear weapons against each other or against nonnuclear countries and nuclear-free zones.[4] When China has raised the
possibility of limited arms control steps, such as the establishment of
nuclear-free zones, it has usually specified NFU pledges as a precondi-
tion or a necessary parallel element. Upon assuming its seat in the
United Nations in November 1971, Peking reiterated its unilateral NFU
pledge and repeated its call for the United States and the Soviet Union
to make similar pledges. The Chinese delegate emphasized that such
pledges could precede a more ambitious program in which an "agreement on non-use of nuclear weapons" should be a first step, to be followed by comprehensive nuclear disarmament involving "complete
prohibition and thorough destruction" of all nuclear weapons, to be discussed at a worldwide summit conference.[5]

It is certainly possible that Peking's interest in NFU pledges stems in
part from a genuine fear that nuclear weapons might be used first
against China by either the United States or the Soviet Union. NFU
pledges by the superpowers would increase the political constraints on
U.S. and Soviet leaders; they would be less likely to consider using
nuclear weapons in times of stress, and in formulating military plans
and developing forces they would be impelled to play down nuclear
options. NFU pledges by the two superpowers would probably make
China less fearful, also, of being intimidated by nuclear threats from
Washington or Moscow.

Thus, support for NFU pledges is an understandable position for
Peking to take and is consistent with China's apparent primary goal of
acquiring nuclear weapons for defensive purposes. At any time in the
foreseeable future, NFU pledges or an NFU agreement would increase
Peking's confidence in the effectiveness of its small nuclear deterrent.
Furthermore, Peking would not face serious strategic costs or problems
from an NFU agreement with other nations, since it has already adopted
this position unilaterally and has little reason to consider initiating the
use of nuclear weapons. In any case, China would retain the capacity
to use nuclear weapons (as would the superpowers, also) and could

4. *Peking Review*, Oct. 23, 1964, p. 6.
5. Speech by Vice Foreign Minister Chiao Kuan-hua at UNGA, Nov. 24,
1971; reported in FBIS, *Daily Report: People's Republic of China*, Nov. 29, 1971,
pp. A22–A24.

always consider doing so in extreme circumstances, whether or not "bound" by an NFU pledge.

The Chinese assert, and may believe, that NFU pledges would be one way for the United States and the USSR to demonstrate nonaggressive intentions and good faith. This is especially important to Peking because of the stresses in its relations with the superpowers in the recent past. During the Ussuri River border clashes in 1969, for instance, Peking may well have feared that Moscow might attack China's strategic facilities with nuclear weapons. Earlier, it probably genuinely feared that the United States was prepared to use nuclear weapons against China at certain times in the middle and late 1950s.

Peking may also believe that without NFU pledges bilateral arms control talks are of little relevance to its interests, and may even threaten them—a view that would militate against Chinese participation in any serious arms control discussions. This point of view is not entirely unreasonable, since partial arms limitation measures of the type already existing or under consideration would do little if anything to reduce the capacity of the United States or the USSR to launch nuclear strikes against China. Given China's small nuclear capability, it is not likely to accept limitations on its force levels, or even its right to conduct nuclear testing, for a number of years. Of the few arms control measures in which the Chinese have shown an interest or which they might consider, they apparently regard NFU pledges as the most important. On the other hand, to the extent that the Chinese are aware of the possible benefits to be obtained from limited arms control measures that are *not* dependent on NFU pledges or major political settlements, they may be using the NFU idea to strengthen their bargaining position; if so, they might be prepared to modify their stance to some degree in the course of negotiations on matters of importance to their interests.

One cannot, of course, rule out the possibility that Peking's position on no first use was adopted primarily for propaganda purposes. Historically, NFU proposals have been advanced by nations that are nonnuclear or weak in nuclear strength, and hence feel vulnerable to nuclear attack; the Soviet Union, for example, expressed interest in the NFU idea at a time when it had only a small nuclear force. From this perspective, insistence on NFU pledges could be conceived by Chinese leaders as a way of placing the United States and the USSR on the defensive or creating problems in relations between the superpowers and their allies—while Peking poses as the leader of the nonnuclear nations.

It is true that much of China's arms control rhetoric has strong propaganda overtones. Its proposals for the total destruction of all nuclear weapons and the preconditions it attaches to the convening of a world disarmament conference cannot at present be taken seriously by the United States and the USSR. (It should be noted, however, that the superpowers themselves put forward broad general disarmament proposals before turning to the practical tasks of finding feasible ways of improving security through limited forms of mutual cooperation.) And Chinese leaders must realize that the United States is unlikely to make an NFU pledge. One cannot exclude the possibility, therefore, that Peking has used the NFU idea, along with demands that the superpowers withdraw all military forces from foreign soil, as a means of *precluding* progress in arms control, while maintaining a peace-seeking image in the world and making no first use a "test" of the sincerity of the superpowers. This might explain why China has stressed the need for global, unqualified NFU pledges on the part of *all* nations possessing nuclear weapons.

This uncertainty about the primary purpose behind Peking's emphasis on NFU pledges makes it difficult to predict how the Chinese would react to a qualified NFU pledge by the United States, either made unilaterally or in the form of a proposed joint statement with China. If the Chinese view their insistence on U.S. and Soviet NFU pledges primarily as a political weapon suited to their relative weakness in strategic nuclear power, they would be likely to denounce any U.S. pledge or proposal that fell short of the unqualified terms they have demanded. On the other hand, they might decide that even a qualified U.S. NFU pledge would increase China's security—either by strengthening the détente with the United States or by reducing the possibility of a U.S. nuclear first strike in the event of a crisis between Peking and Washington. An important purpose of a U.S.–Chinese dialogue on arms control would be to gain a better understanding of the actual reasons why the Chinese have placed such emphasis on NFU pledges.

During the Warsaw meetings in the mid-1960s, Peking made a considerable effort to bring about a discussion of the NFU principle with the U.S. government. In fact, the Chinese proposed in November 1964, shortly after China's first nuclear detonation, that the United States and China each pledge not to use nuclear weapons first against the other. This proposal appears to have been the first made by the Chinese since 1960 that was not conditional on prior U.S. action on the Taiwan issue, which suggests that it was meant seriously. The United States reportedly rejected the measure on the grounds that an NFU agreement would not be enforceable and would not represent a significant contribution to disarmament—neither of which is a persuasive argument against seriously reconsidering the proposition under today's changed conditions.[6] The episode suggests that the Chinese might be receptive to a limited NFU proposal by the United States.

Advantages to the United States of an NFU Pledge

If the Chinese believe that NFU pledges by the superpowers would reduce the threat of nuclear attacks on China, they would presumably see an advantage to China in even a qualified U.S. NFU pledge. But what would be the advantage to the United States?

The first and most important advantage is that it would reduce the likelihood that nuclear weapons will ever again be used in warfare. The farther ahead one looks, the more important this becomes, for the scope of the damage that nuclear weapons could do to the world increases along with the size and number of nuclear arsenals. As Fred Iklé, director of the U.S. Arms Control and Disarmament Agency, has stated: "We should never assume that nuclear weapons could be used without an enormous risk of leading to further nuclear escalation and thus to unprecedented civilian death and suffering."[7] China's arsenal is small today, but as it increases so will U.S. interest in avoiding the risk of nuclear exchange. It is highly desirable, therefore, that the United States and China, as well as other nuclear powers, come increasingly to regard nuclear weapons as usable only to deter the use of such weapons by others, not for responding to conventional attacks. A pledge by the United States not to use nuclear weapons first against China would strengthen the influence of those who take this view of nuclear weapons.

A second advantage, closely allied to the first, is that an NFU pledge would reduce the risk of nuclear proliferation. To the extent that nuclear

6. See *New York Times*, March 12, 1966. See also, *United States–China Relations: A Strategy for the Future*, Hearings before the Subcommittee on Asian and Pacific Affairs of the House Foreign Affairs Committee, 91 Cong. 2 sess. (1970), pp. 313–14; and Kenneth Young, *Negotiating with the Chinese Communists* (McGraw-Hill, 1968), pp. 261–66.

7. Speech delivered to the Joint Harvard–MIT Arms Control Seminar (Feb. 20, 1974; processed).

weapons are regarded only as deterrents, other possible incentives—such as for prestige or as a usable addition to conventional military capacity—for nations to incur the heavy economic and other costs of acquiring nuclear weapons will tend to lose their appeal. The Japanese, for example, most of whom are already strongly committed to the view that Japan should not go nuclear, would be reinforced in that view if the United States were to join China in rejecting first use of nuclear weapons. To them, this action would emphasize the limited value of nuclear weapons and at the same time would demonstrate that the danger of a war that might involve Japan had diminished further.

A third advantage of a U.S. NFU pledge toward China would be to force the United States government to examine critically the contingencies in which it might conceivably want to use nuclear weapons in Asia. In fact, it is almost impossible to imagine situations in which the United States would consider a first strike in Asia to be in its interest. The extremely adverse political consequences and the military risks, to say nothing of moral inhibitions, would impose severe constraints. And the constraints will tend to increase as Chinese capability to launch nuclear weapons against American allies, forces, or even U.S. territory increases. So a good case can be made that a limited NFU pledge toward China would not add significantly to the already considerable constraints on the first use of nuclear weapons by the United States in Asia. An NFU agreement would also have the desirable effect of compelling U.S. defense strategists to consider realistically what conventional forces are required to protect U.S. interests in Asia and to reduce or eliminate any tendency in planning to rely on the nuclear option. This would further diminish the risk that nuclear weapons would ever be used in a crisis between the United States and China. If there should be U.S. interests in Asia that military planners believed could not be defended against conventional attack by U.S. conventional forces, the process of considering an NFU pledge toward China would force a reassessment of whether those interests are so vital that they must be defended by nuclear weapons.

A fourth advantage would be that by responding to China's insistent demand for an NFU pledge as a first step toward other arms control measures, the United States would probably improve prospects for drawing China into serious negotiations on other measures.

Finally, an NFU pledge toward China would constitute an important further step in improving relations with China and thus enhance the prospects for long-term stability in East Asia. By reducing Chinese fears of U.S. intentions it would not only tend to reduce the possibility of a serious military clash with Peking, but also would diminish the danger that any conflict would escalate beyond the nuclear threshold. Conceivably, it might also cause the Chinese to perceive somewhat less need to place high priority on and set high goals for their nuclear program, at least for weapons systems focused primarily on a potential U.S. threat; if so, this would make easier strategic deterrence of China by the United States.

Implications for U.S. Nuclear Defense

A carefully defined and limited NFU pledge by the United States, applied to specified areas, would not impair its capacity to deter China from considering nuclear attacks. If it took the form of a bilateral U.S.–China accord, it would serve to strengthen Peking's self-imposed restraint even as the Chinese nuclear force increases in size. Even a unilateral U.S. pledge conditional on continuance of the Chinese unilateral pledge would have this effect. No special mechanism is needed to ensure that Peking would fulfill its NFU pledge; the United States would simply continue to rely on its retaliatory capacity to deter China's use of nuclear weapons against the United States, its bases, or its allies. A case can be made, in fact, that deterrence against possible nuclear attacks might be strengthened under an NFU arrangement, since reprisals would be more justified.

If an NFU pledge contributed to a reduction in tensions and a productive U.S.–Chinese arms control dialogue, it could decrease the likelihood of nuclear war occurring through mutual miscalculation. This, too, should enhance the effectiveness of our deterrent. For example, if Peking were less fearful of a possible nuclear first strike by the United States in a crisis situation, there would be less chance of a Chinese "panic launch." An NFU pledge would not, of course, prohibit the United States from taking retaliatory action against any missile launch from China, even if accidental or unauthorized.

The nuclear forces of the United States serve at present the purpose not only of deterring the actual use of nuclear weapons by China but also of discouraging China from threatening to use them. Probably no reciprocal or joint NFU pledges could include an explicit prohibition of nuclear threats, since this would be difficult or impossible to formulate, interpret, and verify. But an NFU pledge by the United States—either linked to a renewed Chinese pledge or conditional on continued adherence to the existing pledge—would further decrease the already low propensity of either side to make nuclear threats, since renunciation of first use would make such threats appear less credible as well as inappropriate and inconsistent with the general policies symbolized by a U.S. pledge. An NFU pledge, therefore, should make the United States even less concerned than at present about the possibility of Chinese "rocket rattling," just as it should alleviate Chinese fears of possible U.S. "nuclear coercion."

Disadvantages to the United States of an NFU Pledge

There are, of course, possible disadvantages for the United States in making a no-first-use pledge toward China—principally the cost of denying itself the option of using nuclear weapons to meet a conventional attack and the danger that making the pledge might weaken the confidence of allies in the United States. These disadvantages are less serious, however, than they may seem.

Deterring Conventional Aggression

Some analysts argue that U.S. nuclear strength has helped to deter Chinese conventional aggression in Asia in the past and will continue to do so in the future. This is a debatable point, but to the extent that it is valid, an NFU pledge, by limiting the freedom of the United States to use, or even threaten to use, nuclear weapons to deter or counter Chinese conventional military initiatives, would weaken the effectiveness of the U.S. deterrent. One possible consequence, it could be argued, is a greater readiness on the part of Chinese leaders to consider aggressive moves, whether deliberately planned or arising from unexpected opportunities. At the same time, American leaders might conceivably act with less confidence in situations that could lead to a confrontation with China if the option of using nuclear weapons were unavailable.

It is highly unlikely, however, that in the next ten years the Chinese will take military actions, or even make military threats, that run a high risk of inviting U.S. intervention or retaliation, whether conventional or nuclear. A no-first-use pledge by the United States should not significantly increase Peking's propensity to take higher risk by using its conventional forces abroad, assuming that the United States and its allies in Asia maintain adequate conventional military defense capabilities, along the lines recommended in Chapter 2. Although an NFU pledge would inhibit the United States from using nuclear weapons first in most conceivable situations, the Chinese could not totally rule out the possibility of U.S. nuclear action in extreme circumstances where other military and diplomatic alternatives had failed. However unlikely such a situation might be, Peking would have to be wary of actions that might push the United States to this point. Finally, many factors other than military ones will continue to inhibit the Chinese from considering major conventional military action outside of their borders.

Need for Adequate Conventional Forces

Still, it must be acknowledged that an NFU pledge can be seriously considered by the United States only so long as U.S. and allied conventional forces are capable of meeting potential Chinese threats to vital U.S. interests. If increasing tension and danger of war in East Asia were expected, the United States might find an NFU agreement difficult to accept without boosting the conventional force levels of itself and its allies to meet possible contingencies. But if tensions in the area continue to decline, and particularly if progress could be made toward regional arms control arrangements involving China, the United States might be able to conclude an NFU agreement that would be compatible with a U.S. conventional force level even lower than that now planned.[8]

It must be asked whether, in the wake of the Vietnam experience, it is realistic to expect the American public to support a policy that made an NFU pledge conditional on a given level of conventional forces stationed in or readily deployable to East Asia. It could be argued that popular unwillingness to support such a policy would give the U.S. government no option but to rely on nuclear forces to counter possible Chinese moves. But there is no reason to assume that Americans would prefer using nuclear to conventional weapons in a given situation in East Asia; on the contrary, popular opposition to using nuclear weapons in almost any situation would be very strong. The fundamental problem for the U.S. government is how to limit the use of any form of military

8. For a general discussion of the relationship between conventional force capabilities and NFU accords, see Morton Halperin, "A Proposal for a Ban on the First Use of Nuclear Weapons," *Journal of Arms Control,* vol. 1 (April 1963), pp. 112–22.

force to those situations where the vital nature of U.S. interests can be so clearly demonstrated as to create a strong presumption that essential popular support could be secured. However one may define these vital interests—and definitions will change with changing circumstances— the United States would be wiser to rely on conventional forces for any necessary military confrontation with China than to rely on nuclear weapons, the use of which might well involve unacceptably high costs in terms of U.S. public opinion as in other respects.

Reaction of Allies

Reactions of the Asian allies of the United States to the idea of a U.S. NFU pledge toward China would be mixed, for political as much as or more than for strictly military reasons. Some U.S. allies still fear possible Chinese aggression and expansion, though their fear is generally abating over time. Japan, as has been noted, must concern itself with Peking's nuclear capability. South Korea, Taiwan, and the Southeast Asian nations, in contrast, are primarily concerned about the possibility of a conventional military threat. More generally, Asian nations cannot ignore Peking's growing political influence, which, at least to some extent, is enhanced by the increasing Chinese nuclear arsenal. The new American policy toward China, combined with a lower military profile in Asia and increasing pressures on the U.S. government to avoid military involvement in Asian conflicts, has caused some of our Asian allies to question the dependability of our commitments.

Under unfavorable circumstances, an NFU pledge toward China might reinforce the trends that adversely affect relations with our Asian allies. Although the U.S. guarantee against nuclear attack would remain unaffected, there might be increased anxiety in South Korea and Taiwan in particular that the loss of our "extended deterrent" would weaken the deterrent against Chinese conventional attacks (or, in the case of Korea, North Korean attacks). Further reductions in U.S. ground forces and overall conventional capabilities in Asia would increase this anxiety even more. Even if military analysis could show that there was no cause for increased alarm, some Asians—particularly in Taiwan and South Korea—might view a U.S. NFU pledge as a sign of reduced concern about their security, a portent of "collusion" between the United States and China at the expense of nonnuclear states, or an indication that the political significance of Peking's nuclear power is increasing—three political trends that could enhance Chinese influence in Asia.

Such an adverse impact would, however, be mitigated by the provision that the pledge would be nullified by Chinese use of nuclear weapons against the territory or forces of a U.S. ally. Moreover, it is doubtful that the Asian allies of the United States rely heavily on the assumption that the United States would use nuclear weapons to counter nonnuclear attacks against them. When the Chinese acquire ICBMs, the suspicion will grow that in crisis situations the United States would not be prepared to "risk San Francisco" to save cities in Asia. Furthermore, most leaders in Asian countries allied to the United States recognize that full-scale nuclear war could destroy their nations, so that they would almost certainly be reluctant to see the United States actually use nuclear weapons. Small nations on the Asian mainland would probably oppose the use of even tactical nuclear weapons on the battlefield because of the resulting destruction. In many respects, therefore, an NFU agreement would simply "codify" an already perceived reality.

Because of the vital importance to the United States of its relations with Japan, the possible effect on Japan of a U.S. NFU pledge toward China should be carefully weighed. Given the current climate of declining tension in East Asia, most Japanese would probably welcome such a pledge. There is some danger, however, that it would reduce the Japanese government's confidence in the U.S. defense commitment to Japan or that the opposition in Japan would be able to exploit it to strengthen pressures against the U.S.–Japan security treaty, arguing that tensions in Asia had diminished to the point where Japan no longer needed the treaty. It would thus be essential to gain in advance the support of the Japanese government for the NFU concept. The potential gains from an NFU pledge toward China would not justify the risk of serious differences on a basic security issue with the most important U.S. Asian ally.

By discussing thoroughly the purposes and implications of an NFU agreement and demonstrating an intention to maintain a strong conventional military capability in the region, or rapidly transferable to it, the United States could minimize the potential anxieties of its smaller Asian allies. Moreover, a bilateral U.S.–Chinese NFU accord could diminish allied fears that Peking might use nuclear weapons for aggressive or coercive purposes, and this might generally reduce concern over the risk of nuclear war erupting in Asia. Indeed, the fact that the United States had agreed to make an NFU pledge within the framework of an arms control dialogue with China—especially if it were associated with other agreements that could enhance security in Asia—could help to create a confidence in the political climate that might substantially reduce the fear of Chinese aggression.

Our allies in Europe might react negatively to a U.S. NFU pledge, even one made with respect to China only, on the grounds that it would set a precedent that would exert pressure on the United States to make a similar pledge with respect to the USSR—a step that, in the eyes of many Europeans, would endanger their security. A strongly negative European reaction probably would outweigh the advantages to the United States of an NFU pledge toward China. But it would be hoped that Europeans would recognize that the problems of security in Europe differ greatly from those in Asia. They might be brought to see that the proposed pledge made sense in the context of U.S. policy toward Asia and need not have undesirable repercussions on the U.S. commitment to the defense of Europe.

Soviet Reactions

A U.S. pledge toward China might raise some issues affecting U.S.–Soviet as well as Sino-Soviet relations. Moscow has formally advocated a nonuse convention to be signed by all states, which would require all signatories not to use or threaten to use nuclear weapons and not to encourage other nations to do so.[9] The Soviets have argued that such a convention would reduce the risks of nuclear war, eliminate incentives to acquire nuclear weapons, and facilitate progress toward general disarmament. This proposal was supported by the East European nations, the UAR, and India. However, although Khrushchev once stated that the Soviet Union would never be the first to "set nuclear rockets in motion," and Podgorny told a Japanese politician that the Soviet Union would not use nuclear weapons before other nations use them, the USSR has not formally forsworn the first-use option.[10]

The Russians would undoubtedly have mixed feelings about a unilateral U.S. NFU pledge toward China or an NFU agreement with China, and it seems fair to assume that the formal nonuse proposal was motivated mainly by propaganda considerations. In 1964, it is true, the Soviet Union approved of Peking's NFU position, but in the context of

9. For the Soviet position on this point, see U.S. Department of State, *Documents on Disarmament, 1968* (September 1969), pp. 706–07.

10. *Tokyo Shimbun,* Jan. 20, 1972.

current Sino-Soviet relations it is difficult to imagine that the USSR is eager to make an NFU pledge toward China.[11] A U.S.–China NFU arrangement could put pressure on the Russians to consider such a possibility, however. If China insisted on a Soviet as well as a U.S. pledge, it could, of course, prevent any U.S.–China accord, although not a unilateral U.S. pledge.

Conceivably, however, the Soviet Union might use the precedent of a U.S.–China NFU agreement to propose an NFU agreement between NATO and the Warsaw Pact that would include a bilateral U.S.–Soviet NFU agreement affecting their home territories and forces. Moscow might also insist on British and French participation, even if it recognized that their approval would be unlikely. The Kremlin might, in short, press such a proposal primarily to create difficulties among western allies.

Reactions of Nonnuclear Nations

In general, many nonnuclear nations could be expected to have mixed feelings toward an NFU agreement involving China. In some cases they might feel that the potential benefits associated with a lowered risk of nuclear threats would be counterbalanced by a weakening of the credibility of U.S. (or Soviet) deterrence against the possibility of conventional Chinese military threats. Other, more sophisticated, nations, with experience in arms control and security matters, might tend to view an NFU agreement as only marginally useful, and therefore perhaps not worth seeking. Some might criticize China for insisting on NFU pledges before showing any willingness to cooperate in other nuclear arms control arrangements, such as the NPT, the limited test ban, and SALT. Nevertheless, many nonnuclear nations would probably react favorably to a U.S.–Chinese NFU arrangement, not only because it would represent one further step toward arms control, but also because it would involve China in the negotiating process.

Conclusions

The potential long-term advantages of a U.S. NFU pledge toward China—reducing the risk of nuclear war and nuclear proliferation,

11. See Chapter 6 for a discussion of possible Soviet reaction to an NFU declaration tied to a multilateral agreement on Korea.

compelling critical examination of U.S. policy on the use of nuclear weapons in Asia, furthering the improvement of U.S. relations with China, and enhancing the prospects of involving China in arms control negotiations—justify its serious consideration by the United States. An examination of the contingencies in Asia in which the United States might consider using nuclear weapons against conventional attack (the principal rationale for maintaining the option of first use) suggests that an NFU pledge toward China would add little to the existing constraints on the United States. A strong adverse reaction by U.S. allies, however —especially the Japanese or Western Europeans—probably would largely cancel out the potential advantages of the pledge. Consequently, it would be essential to gain the support, or at least the acquiescence, of major U.S. allies. Discussion of the topic among private citizens of the nations concerned would be a useful means of drawing public attention to it and thus preparing the ground for official discussions among governments.

CHAPTER SIX

Arms Control in Korea

The United States, working with both allies and adversaries, is engaged in a difficult, long-term endeavor to build a more peaceful and stable international order in East Asia. There is no part of this region where the attainment of long-term stability is both so difficult and so vital as it is in Korea, where important interests of China, the Soviet Union, Japan, and the United States all converge. The two governments in Korea, one closely associated with the United States and Japan, the other with the USSR and China, and both of them heavily armed, are antagonistic and suspicious toward each other. Any armed conflict between them would entail grave danger of big-power involvement.

Since the Korean war, the United States has assumed special responsibilities in Korea, including a defense commitment to South Korea backed up by U.S. troops stationed there. This commitment is an important adjunct of the U.S. security treaty with Japan, for most Japanese consider the security of the Republic of Korea to be closely related to Japan's own security. Since Japanese participation is essential to creating a peaceful and stable world order, maintaining a cooperative and productive relationship with Japan is the first priority for the United States in East Asia. If Japan were to lose confidence in the U.S. defense commitment, drift away from association with the United States, and rearm massively with nuclear weapons, East Asia would become less stable and U.S. security could be endangered.

Consequently, it is important to the United States to find ways of ensuring the long-term stability of Korea, both to protect the U.S. relationship with Japan and to reduce the risk of a military conflict in Korea that could explode into war among the big powers. The last several years have seen reduced tension among the four big powers and lower risk of war on the peninsula, but these trends could easily be reversed. It is important to find additional ways of maintaining this desirable momentum.

Prospects for Enhancing Stability in Korea

The prospects for further progress in making Korea more stable are encouraging in one important respect: none of the four big powers with interests in Korea appears inclined to run high risks in order to bring about the reunification of Korea under the government it supports. All seem to prefer to live with a divided Korea rather than face the dangers and uncertainties that would accompany an attempt to reunify it by military force.

Recent trends toward declining tension between the United States and China, the United States and the USSR, Japan and the USSR, and Japan and China have reinforced the inclination of the big powers to avoid military conflict over Korea. Moreover, these trends—and especially the impact of President Nixon's dramatic visit to China—helped to set in motion talks between North Korea and South Korea for the first time since the Korean war.[1] Meetings between the Red Cross societies of the two Koreas for the purpose of arranging reunions of families separated by the division of Korea were agreed upon in August 1971, soon after President Nixon announced his intention to visit China. Then, in July 1972, officials of the two Koreas announced agreement on certain principles for reunification: that unification should be achieved by Koreans without outside interference; that it should be achieved by peaceful means, not by the use of force; that neither side would defame the other or engage in armed provocations, and that both would take mea-

1. For evidence of the close connection between the changing international environment (especially the improvement of U.S. relations with China and the USSR and Sino-Japanese relations) and the changing policies of the two Koreas toward each other, see particularly Premier Kim Chong-pil's speech of Nov. 15, 1972, on constitutional revision (reported in Foreign Broadcast Information Service [FBIS], *Daily Report: East Asia,* Nov. 21, 1972, pp. E1–E8); the *Special Commentary on President Park Chung-hee's Special Statement Regarding Foreign Policy for Peace and Unification* (Seoul: Korea Information Service, June 1973); and Premier Kim Chong-pil's statement of June 23, 1973 (reported in FBIS, *Daily Report: East Asia,* June 26, 1973, pp. E1–E7). North Korean public statements do not link the new moves between North and South Korea with the changing international situation, but Pyongyang's actions imply a close relationship.

sures to prevent inadvertent military incidents; that various exchanges would be carried out in many fields; that both would cooperate positively in the Red Cross talks; that a direct telephone "hot line" would be installed between Seoul and Pyongyang; and that a North-South coordinating committee would be established to solve various problems between the two sides and to settle the unification problem on the basis of the foregoing principles.[2]

Although the North-South coordinating committee was established and the hot line installed pursuant to the July 1972 agreement, as of early 1975 neither the meetings of this committee nor those of the Red Cross societies had made perceptible progress, whether toward the unification of Korea, the reunion of families, or, indeed, toward any form of peaceful interaction between the two sides. Both sets of talks appeared to be stalemated and the positions of the two sides were far apart. The dialogue was not broken off, but North and South continued to view one another with great hostility and suspicion. In these still dangerous circumstances, the United States must decide how best to conduct its relations with the other big powers concerned and with the two Koreas so as to edge Pyongyang and Seoul toward genuine dialogue and to further a reduction in the tension between them.

Proposed International Agreements

A possible means of diminishing the risk of war in Korea and improving the chances for progress in the negotiations between the two Koreas is to strengthen what may already be a tacit understanding among the four big powers that conflict in Korea would benefit none of them. It might be argued that now that Seoul and Pyongyang have begun to talk, the big powers should refrain from attempting any arrangement regarding Korea for fear of upsetting or stalling these talks. This is a danger that would have to be guarded against. The big powers should not become involved in the negotiations between North and South; these should continue "without outside interference" as the principles of unification provide. But it must be remembered that these negotiations would probably never have begun had it not been for the climate created by improved relations among the big powers.

A suitable format for international agreements aimed at reducing the

2. *Washington Post*, July 4, 1972.

risk of war in Korea would be a basic agreement between the two Koreas, endorsed by the four major powers, which would also subscribe to undertakings of their own concerning their actions toward Korea. The agreements could contain two basic elements: the renunciation of force and the establishment of a nuclear-free zone.

Renunciation of Force

The two Korean governments would renounce the use of military force against each other. This would be the basic agreement to which the others would be linked. The two Koreas have already gone a considerable distance in this direction by including in the principles for unification provisions that unification should be achieved by peaceful means, not by the use of force, and that neither side would engage in armed provocations. Moreover, Kim Il-song has proposed a "peace agreement" between the two Koreas, conditional upon the withdrawal of U.S. forces from South Korea; while Park Chung-hee has countered with a proposal for a "non-aggression agreement" that would provide for continuance of the Military Armistice Agreement and would include pledges to refrain from interfering in each other's internal affairs.[3] Thus, both have declared their willingness in principle to renounce the use of force against each other, although they disagree sharply on the necessary conditions for entering into formal undertakings to this end. For this to be made part of an international arrangement would require a formal instrument renouncing the use of force, which, in turn, would require a more widely accepted international status for both governments. This seems to be evolving, but it may be some time before the process is complete.

In a separate agreement, the four big powers would endorse the renunciation of force by the two Koreas and, in consideration of that agreement, would themselves agree to refrain from the use of force in Korea. The favorable climate for an explicit renunciation of force toward Korea was heightened by President Nixon's visits to Peking and Moscow and the resulting agreements by both sides—in the Shanghai communiqué and the Moscow declaration of principles—that they would not resort to the threat or use of force in their relations with each other.

3. See *New Year Press Conference by President Park Chung-hee, January 18, 1974*, Korea Policy Series, no. 18 (Korean Overseas Information Service, January 1974), pp. 28, 29; and response in *Nodong Sinmun* editorial, Jan. 26, 1974 (quoted in FBIS, *Daily Report: East Asia*, Jan. 28, 1974, pp. D1–D6).

Similar language appears in the communiqué signed by Premiers Tanaka and Chou in September 1972. The way has thus been paved, in a sense, for applying these principles in a concrete situation where danger of big-power conflict exists.

Although Kim Il-song provides for renunciation of force in his proposed bilateral peace agreement, he might be reluctant to see this agreement tied to a four-power accord; he might fear that this would make him subject to constraints from his allies (which, of course, would be a purpose of the arrangement). It seems doubtful, however, that this consideration alone would make it possible for Kim to block the agreements if they had considerable appeal to China and the USSR.

Nuclear-Free Zone

The second element in this set of agreements would be a declaration by the two Koreas that their territories would constitute a nuclear-free zone. Each would undertake not to manufacture or possess nuclear weapons, or allow them into its territory. The four big powers would endorse this declaration, agree to respect the status of Korea as a nuclear-free zone, and agree not to use nuclear weapons against Korean territory.

This provision of the proposed set of agreements might have particular appeal to China, as it would create on its border the first of what the Chinese might hope would become a growing number of "zones of peace" such as they have proposed. Although the actual military significance to China of the removal from Korean territory of U.S. nuclear weapons would not be great, the psychological and political implications could be important. From the Chinese viewpoint, one of the greatest values of such an agreement would be the probable strengthening of opposition in Japan to remilitarization; the nuclear-free zone in Korea might thus be seen as the first step toward an expanded nuclear-free zone that would include Japan.

Although the United States (and South Korea) would seem to be making important concessions in agreeing to the removal of U.S. nuclear weapons from South Korea, this action in itself would not significantly inhibit the United States from resorting to nuclear weapons in fulfilling its commitment to help defend Korea against attack (in the absence, of course, of a no-first-use pledge toward China). Any attack would violate the interlocking set of agreements, thus releasing all parties from their pledges. The United States would be handicapped only to the extent that it could not have nuclear weapons positioned in Korea in advance, but they could still be carried aboard ships in the Pacific as insurance against violation of the agreements. In any case, since the political costs of the actual use of U.S. nuclear weapons in Korea would be extremely high, by agreeing to respect Korea as a nuclear-free zone, the United States would be giving up an option it is most unlikely ever to use.

International agreement on a nuclear-free zone in Korea would also serve other U.S. interests. It should tend to strengthen the disposition of the Japanese to remain nonnuclear. It might prove to be the first breakthrough in involving the Chinese in serious limited arms control negotiations. And it would be of great symbolic importance as establishing the first nuclear-free zone in Asia, thus expanding the concept of the nuclear-free zone beyond Latin America.

A four-power agreement on Korea may seem to be unrealistic in light of the complications posed by the hostility between North and South Korea and the serious differences between China and the USSR. Of course, formal agreements are not the only possible way to improve the international climate as it affects Korea and to diminish the risk of open conflict there. Bilateral discussions and arrangements among the four powers could also serve to reinforce their shared perception that conflict in Korea would not be in the interest of any. Strengthening tacit understandings in this regard could turn out to be the most that can be achieved in the next few years. But even that goal is more likely to be reached if serious thought is given to the possibilities of explicit agreements.

A fundamental requirement for the United States in seeking international arrangements would be that they be supported by Japan, as well as by South Korea, and not in any way weaken Japanese confidence in the U.S. defense commitment to Japan. The proposed agreements might create internal political difficulties for the Japanese government, for reasons given below. Hence, it would be essential for the U.S. and Japanese governments to agree on a plan of action and to consult closely with each other at each stage in carrying it out.

A set of agreements such as the one proposed here would present many problems to each of the six governments involved; they undoubtedly would require numerous refinements and amendments. Yet, since all four big powers have a common interest in avoiding conflict over Korea, it is not impossible that they could work out arrangements, either in formal agreements or in private understandings, that would serve all their interests.

The Chinese Viewpoint

Given that China is likely to be defense oriented through the 1970s (as explored in Chapter 1), there is little reason to suppose that the Chinese would welcome attempts to reunify Korea by means that involved high risk and heavy burdens for China. On the contrary, recent Chinese statements of support for North Korea emphasize the desirability of unifying Korea peacefully.

The Chinese might even see an advantage for them in a Korea that remained divided for a considerable period, although they could not afford to admit it. So long as Korea is divided, the freedom of action of each part is limited by its obsession with the confrontation between the two parts and the problem of reunification. North Korea's dependence on Moscow and Peking, though permitting some leeway for playing off one against the other, does limit Pyongyang's freedom of action. A united Korea could, like Yugoslavia, follow a more independent policy and could develop counterbalancing relations with the United States and Japan.

Whatever may be the true Chinese attitude toward Korean reunification, there are other reasons why a relatively stable situation in the Korean peninsula would be more in China's interest than a state of rising tension threatening open conflict. First, the Chinese have a considerable stake, just as the United States does, in the newly improved Sino-American relations. Serious trouble in Korea would upset Peking's careful maneuvering to strengthen its position against Soviet pressure. Second, the Chinese are concerned about Japan's growing economic strength, its increasing influence in South Korea, and the possibility that Japan will again become a major military power. Conflict in Korea might well strengthen U.S.–Japanese relations and accelerate Japanese rearmament. Moreover, possession of a small nuclear force is unlikely to make the Chinese more aggressive toward Korea. Finally, if international arrangements were agreed upon to make Korea a nuclear-free zone, the Chinese could claim credit for the idea as a response to their appeal at the United Nations for the establishment of "zones of peace."

For all these reasons, a set of international agreements—participated in by the four big powers whose interests intersect in the Korean peninsula—that diminished the risk of military conflict there might be of substantial interest to the Chinese.

The Soviet Viewpoint

The Russians, like the Chinese, do not appear to regard the unification of Korea under Pyongyang as so important a national interest that they would be prepared to assume serious risks or heavy costs to achieve it. The behavior of the USSR at the time of the *Pueblo* and EC-121 incidents unmistakably demonstrated a Soviet desire not to see the danger of conflict grow.

The Russians might be more inclined to accept an international agreement on Korea than the Chinese because they would see it as a check on the kind of Chinese adventurism that could conceivably draw the Soviet Union into undesired conflict with the United States. Some Soviet leaders regard the Chinese as unpredictable, subject to irrational behavior (as during the Cultural Revolution), and more inclined to take risks than the Russians. As the principal supplier of arms to North Korea, the Soviet Union would have to assume a substantial burden in military aid if conflict broke out, as occurred in the Vietnam war. The deep Soviet suspicion of the Chinese and the maneuvering for advantage that has taken place over the years between the two nations in respect to both Vietnam and Korea would incline the Soviets to suspect that, under certain circumstances, the Chinese might gamble that damage to U.S.–Soviet relations arising from a renewed confrontation over Korea would outweigh any damage to their own relations with the United States. The Russians would thus tend to favor international arrangements that stabilize Korea and make it more difficult for the Chinese to urge or acquiesce in provocative actions by North Korea.

Another important reason why the Soviet Union might favor international arrangements to stabilize Korea is that such arrangements would probably create a better atmosphere for the cultivation of relations with Japan. Rising tension in Korea would disturb the Japanese. It would cause the Japanese left to raise a clamor against South Korea and the United States for causing the tension, which might be favorable to Soviet aims in Japan. On the other hand, the government and conservative elements in Japan would be concerned about Japanese security and the protection of Japanese trade and investment in South Korea; this might well cause South Korea, Japan, and the United States to draw closer together. Yet another possibility is that, under certain circumstances (and especially if relations between the United States and Japan had deteriorated considerably), the main reaction in Japan could be isolationist—a desire not to become involved.

Thus, although it is difficult to predict just where the weight of Japanese reaction to rising tension in Korea would fall, it would be hard for a Soviet policymaker to assume with confidence that it would improve Soviet relations with Japan. Even if it strained U.S.–Japanese relations, it would not necessarily mean better relations between Japan and the USSR. Given the long-standing Japanese dislike of Russians, and the fact that the USSR would have to back North Korea against South Korea in order to maintain its influence in Pyongyang in competition with China, it seems probable that a Korean conflict would make it harder, not easier, for Moscow to cultivate Tokyo.

One aspect of Soviet-Japanese relations would seem particularly to favor Soviet interest in preventing conflict in Korea—that is the Soviet desire for large-scale Japanese investment in long-term projects for the development of natural resources in Siberia. Instability and international tension in Northeast Asia would impair the prospects for such investment.

If one assumes, then, that (1) improving Soviet-Japanese relations at the expense of Sino-Japanese and U.S.–Japanese relations has a higher priority for the USSR than any conceivable objective in Korea; and (2) that the Russians believe that, on balance, rising tension in Korea would make improvement of Soviet-Japanese relations more difficult; the USSR might well consider its interest to lie in support for an international arrangement that made open conflict in Korea less likely.

The Japanese Viewpoint

Korea is important to Japan in several ways. As Premier Sato declared in the Nixon-Sato communiqué of November 1969, the Japanese government regards the security of the Republic of Korea as "essential to Japan's own security." Even though domestic political contention in

Japan has tended to diminish the importance of this specific clause—
in part because Sato's name is attached to it—the importance of Korea
to Japan has not diminished. Japan has a large and rapidly growing
economic stake in South Korea. Furthermore, how the United States is
seen as fulfilling its defense commitment to South Korea will influence
significantly Japanese appraisal of the reliability of the U.S. defense
commitment to Japan.

The majority of Japanese would welcome international arrangements
to reduce the risk of war in Korea. Action that relaxed tension and improved stability in Northeast Asia would provide more solid ground for
their conviction that military strength should not have a larger role in
Japanese foreign policy; it would suit their desire for Japan to play a
more active role in world politics by means of "peace diplomacy." There
would be substantial opposition, however, to an agreement that committed Japan in any way to possible military action in Korea. Thus,
Japan could join in renouncing the use of force in Korea or in agreeing
to respect a nuclear-free zone there, but not in guaranteeing the territorial integrity of the two Koreas or any other formula that might call on
the guarantors to undertake military action.

Public debate in Japan on the terms of possible international arrangements for Korea could create problems for the Japanese government.
The opposition and a large part of the information media would probably support North Korean insistence on total withdrawal of U.S. forces
from Korea, and possibly North Korean demands on other issues that
would be unacceptable to the United States. The domestic debate might
well put a strain on relations between the governments of Japan and
South Korea, as well as providing opportunities for the Chinese or the
Russians to exploit in an attempt to strengthen their influence on Japan.
If an international agreement were reached, many Japanese might
assume that the danger of war had been totally removed, which would
strengthen opposition to the U.S.–Japan security treaty. All these considerations underline again the importance of the closest consultation
between the United States and Japan throughout negotiations with the
other governments concerned on measures to reduce the danger of conflict in Korea.

The North Korean Viewpoint

North Korea's fundamental policy aim has been to get U.S. forces
withdrawn from South Korea, and it has been supported in this position

by China and the USSR. Consequently, Pyongyang would be inclined to favor an international agreement that required the withdrawal of U.S. forces but did not provide for any international intervention in Korea that could limit its freedom of action in seeking control over the South. Kim Il-song has consistently rejected a role for the United Nations in Korea or, indeed, any other form of restrictive international supervision. He calls for resolution of the Korean problem by the Koreans themselves without outside interference. He accepted the Neutral Nations Supervisory Commission,[4] but its composition and rules of procedure guaranteed a stalemate on any significant issue, and its movements in North Korea were severely restricted.

Kim Il-song has shown an imaginative flexibility in the proposals he has made on the reunification of Korea. He had succeeded through his "peace offensive" in placing the South Korean government on the diplomatic defensive until Park Chung-hee boldly seized the initiative in June 1973 by calling for the admission of both Korean governments to the United Nations as a provisional measure until reunification could be achieved. Kim denounced this proposal as a device to perpetuate the division of Korea and the presence of U.S. forces in South Korea. He did, however, send an observer delegation to New York to participate along with the South Korean observer delegation in the UN discussion of the Korean issue in the autumn of 1973. Moreover, North Korea has entered other UN-affiliated international bodies alongside South Korea and has accepted diplomatic relations with countries that also maintain relations with the South. Clearly, enhancing its standing in the international community is an important objective for North Korea. Thus, Kim could be expected to react to the idea of international agreements on Korea in ways that made him appear forthcoming, but did not in any way divert him from his major objectives of getting U.S. forces out of Korea and rendering ineffectual any international bodies that might limit his freedom of action.

Even though Kim opposed provisions favored by the United States and South Korea, he probably would not be opposed in principle to international negotiations, which would enhance Pyongyang's international status. And so long as North Korea was involved in negotiations, it would be less likely than otherwise to resort to military force.

4. The Neutral Nations Supervisory Commission, composed of representatives from Sweden, Switzerland, Poland, and Czechoslovakia, was established by the Korean armistice agreement of July 27, 1953, to supervise provisions of the agreement.

The South Korean Viewpoint

The South Koreans, having been overrun by North Korea in the past, are obsessed with the need for military defense against possible renewed attack from the North. They are particularly worried about the exposed position of Seoul—much closer to the border than Pyongyang and home for 20 percent of South Korea's population. They fear a sudden thrust to seize a piece of South Korean territory, perhaps even Seoul itself, followed by a call for a cease-fire in place that they fear would be overwhelmingly supported by world opinion. They note the success of the Israelis in seizing and holding territory and the successful defeat by the Indian army of the Pakistanis in Bangla Desh, and above all the inability of the United Nations to do anything to change situations created by military force.

For South Koreans the lesson to be learned from recent history is that they must rely on their own military force, backed up by the United States to the extent the United States can be relied on. Hence, there would be deep suspicion in South Korea that international arrangements would serve only to weaken their power to resist invasion and the ability and willingness of the United States to back them. They would place little confidence in pledges by North Korea, China, or the Soviet Union to refrain from use of force. They would be especially suspicious if the main objective of the communist powers appeared to be the withdrawal of U.S. forces from South Korea in exchange for promises.

If the South Korean government could have confidence that the international arrangement would, in fact, reduce the risk of war, it would have strong reason to favor it. Some military leaders might look with disfavor on developments that could cause a reduction of military forces, and other members of the southern leadership might fear that a less militant atmosphere would endanger their political power. Nevertheless, many in the South would recognize that South Korea had much to gain from reduced threat of war. The obsessive fear of attack from the North weakens confidence in the ability of the larger South to cope with the highly disciplined, strictly controlled society of North Korea. If the military element were deemphasized, the demonstrated success of South Korea in economic development and international trade would be more in evidence and strengthen the confidence of South Koreans that time works in their favor. Moreover, the greater stability in Korea and reduced risk of conflict afforded by international arrangements would increase the attractiveness of the South to foreign investors and thus facilitate the inflow of outside capital essential to South Korea's rapid economic development. Thus, South Koreans would not necessarily oppose international arrangements in principle—but they would have to be persuaded that they would work as intended.[5]

The Question of U.S. Forces in Korea

Although the set of agreements described above, incorporating the concepts of renunciation of force and a nuclear-free zone, would have some attraction for all the big powers by reducing the possibility of conflict, a serious obstacle to agreement would be North Korean demands, supported by the USSR and China, for the total withdrawal of U.S. troops from South Korea. This demand would be bitterly opposed by South Korea.

Pyongyang would probably take an intransigent position on its demand for withdrawal of U.S. troops, not only because it would hope to use the pressures for international agreement on Korea as leverage on the United States but also because it would not want to enter into a nuclear-free zone agreement that did not provide for U.S. withdrawal. An international agreement on a nuclear-free zone, consented to by the two Koreas, that did not provide for withdrawal of all U.S. forces would appear to approve tacitly the continued presence of U.S. conventional forces in the South. Thus, North Korea would be likely to condemn a U.S. proposal for renunciation of force and a nuclear-free zone as a trick intended to gain international acceptance of U.S. forces in South Korea.

Although the Chinese would support the North Korean position— for not to do so would cause them to lose ground to the USSR in Pyongyang—their support might be only lukewarm because of their special concern about the Japanese. It is worth noting that Chou En-lai, when stating that "American troops should all be withdrawn" from

5. Although in July 1972 Premier Kim Chong-pil rejected a proposal by the political opposition in South Korea for an international guarantee of the security of Korea by the United States, the Soviet Union, China, and Japan, the South Korean government would be less likely to reject a well-prepared proposal supported by the United States and Japan. Reported in FBIS, *Daily Report: Asia and Pacific,* July 18, 1972.

Korea, almost immediately added that "the Korean question is also linked up with the problem of Japanese militarism. If things do not go well, Japan might use the treaty it has concluded with South Korea, i.e., the Japan–R.O.K. treaty, to get into South Korea immediately upon withdrawal of U.S. forces."[6] The Chinese concern about Japanese militarism may have diminished as a result of the successful visit by Tanaka to Peking, which resulted in an agreement on normalization of relations between Japan and China, but it has not vanished. How staunchly the Chinese supported North Korean demands for total withdrawal of U.S. forces would thus depend on their judgment of the chances that the Japanese might eventually move into the vacated spot. It would also be affected by Chinese concern that a decline in U.S. military strength in Northeast Asia would enhance Soviet influence and freedom of action there. China's leaders have made no secret of their approval of the U.S.–Japan security pact for that very reason. China might be amenable to a U.S. withdrawal over a considerable period of time, or even to leaving open the date for final withdrawal, so long as the United States agreed in principle to withdraw. In the same interview with Reston, Chou En-lai referred to the withdrawal of foreign troops as a question of principle, but said that timing and method were matters to be agreed upon by the countries concerned.

Although the Russians would not like to see U.S. forces replaced by Japanese forces in South Korea, they seem less concerned about that possibility than the Chinese. They would therefore be inclined to endorse Pyongyang's view of the importance of total U.S. withdrawal, both on general principles and in order not to lose influence to China in North Korea. It would suit general Soviet interests not to have U.S. troops in an area so close to the Soviet frontier, even though the small U.S. force in South Korea poses no significant threat to the USSR.

In short, it is probable that all the communist nations would denounce the continued presence of U.S. forces in South Korea as inconsistent with a U.S. pledge to renounce the use of force in Korea. They could argue also that so long as the United States had military bases and forces in South Korea, it would be impossible to verify whether the United States was, in fact, complying with the provisions of the nuclear-free zone agreement. In support of this they could point to U.S. resistance to demands by the Japanese left wing for physical verification of the withdrawal of U.S. nuclear weapons from Okinawa.

6. In an interview with James Reston, *New York Times*, Aug. 10, 1971.

Japanese reaction to pressures for the removal of all U.S. forces from South Korea would be mixed. The Japan Socialist Party and other opposition parties would push for withdrawal. They would argue that the pledges by all six powers to renounce force would adequately protect South Korea so there would no longer be any need for U.S. forces there. Most members of the Liberal Democratic Party, on the other hand, would be uneasy about the idea of total withdrawal. They see the presence of U.S. forces in South Korea, bolstering the U.S. pledge to help defend South Korea if attacked, as making it unnecessary for Japan to assume the burden of assuring the security of the South. They would have much less confidence in renunciation of force pledges by the communist powers than would the Japanese left wing. Yet the Japanese government would find it difficult to explain convincingly to the Japanese public why U.S. troops would still be needed in South Korea once the four big powers had agreed to a renunciation of force and a nuclear-free zone there.

South Koreans would take the North Korean insistence on total withdrawal of U.S. forces as evidence of bad faith. They would tend to assume that the North Koreans did not intend to observe their pledge to renounce force, and wanted to get the U.S. forces out of the way to improve their chances of conquering the South. Even if the United States believed that North Korea would be deterred from attacking the South by the four-power agreement, together with the prospect that U.S. forces would return to South Korea if conflict arose, it would be difficult to convince the South Koreans of this. Their deep suspicion and fear of the North and the uncertainty whether U.S. forces would indeed be returned in a crisis would lead them to oppose vigorously international arrangements that involved total withdrawal of U.S. forces. South Korean leaders are realistic enough, however, to recognize that they cannot expect U.S. forces to remain indefinitely and have begun publicly preparing their people for the possibility of U.S. withdrawal by stressing the need for Korean self-reliance.[7]

The United States, after its experience in 1950, would also be justified in feeling skeptical about Kim Il-sung's intentions. Even though the proposed interlocking agreements might indeed cause the Soviet Union and China to place some restraint on reckless action by Kim, there could be no assurance as to how firmly they would or could control

7. See statements by President Park and Premier Kim cited in note 1, above.

him once the United States had totally withdrawn its forces. Kim might assume that, after the Vietnam experience, the chances were slight that the United States would again intervene militarily on the Asian mainland.

Although the differences among the powers over the presence of U.S. forces in South Korea would make agreement on the proposed international arrangements difficult, the progress made so far in improving U.S. relations with Moscow and Peking opens the door to other possible agreements in other situations where the big powers perceive some common interest. The position taken by the United States in the Shanghai communiqué on its forces in Taiwan provides a precedent for agreeing in principle to total withdrawal of forces from an area, while retaining the right to determine when relaxation of tensions justifies actual withdrawal. A similar formula conceivably might be acceptable to China and the USSR in Korea, especially in view of Peking's concern that the Japanese military might move in when the U.S. military moved out. After all, there would be advantages to both Moscow and Peking in getting the United States to agree to a nuclear-free zone in Korea even without a firm date for withdrawal of all its conventional forces. While Pyongyang would be harder to convince than Peking, if both North Korea's big-power allies saw important advantages in the proposed agreements, they might be able to persuade Pyongyang to accept the U.S. commitment in principle to withdraw its forces.

The United States could make a strong case for its insistence on retaining the right to determine the timing of the withdrawal of its forces. It could point out that it had already withdrawn a substantial number of forces from South Korea and that the relaxation of tension resulting from agreement on renunciation of force and the nuclear-free zone would permit the withdrawal of more, but that it would be unreasonable to expect total withdrawal until the two Koreas had come to have greater confidence in each other. That the United States is at a geographical disadvantage compared to Pyongyang's allies justifies South Korea's desire for keeping a small U.S. force on hand. The United States would be offering a significant concession by agreeing to deny itself the military advantage of having nuclear weapons stationed in Korea, while China and the USSR retain the right to station their own nuclear-armed forces on their own territory near the Korean border.

Before agreeing in principle to total withdrawal, the United States would have to reassure South Korea and Japan that it did not intend to withdraw until tension had genuinely decreased to the point where the U.S. military presence in South Korea was no longer needed. One means of reassuring the South Koreans would be to agree to supply the weapons that they consider necessary for defense against the North, thereby permitting the gradual withdrawal of U.S. forces without seeming to prejudice the security of the South. Unfortunately, the tension and suspicion that exist in Korea today will incline both sides to overestimate their military needs, even if neither side really intends to mount a large-scale attack on the other. American assistance in equipping South Korean forces at the level they regard as necessary for their defense would thus tend to spur the North Koreans to demand more help from Moscow and Peking, thereby accelerating the arms race on the peninsula.

To the extent that Korean anxiety about the withdrawal of U.S. forces could be allayed by assurances that the United States was able and willing to return its forces to the area quickly in an emergency, pressures from the South Koreans for more equipment could be eased. Joint planning and standby bases kept in readiness for U.S. forces, bolstered by occasional exercises involving the rapid deployment of U.S. forces to South Korea, could go far to substitute for the actual presence of substantial numbers of troops, although these measures would inevitably be somewhat less effective—both as a deterrent to the North and an assurance to the South—than U.S. forces regularly present. Arrangements for the emergency return of U.S. air force units would be particularly appropriate, both because it is in the air that South Korea is weakest relative to the North and because air units could be brought in most quickly.

International Supervision of the Demilitarized Zone

Another means of assuring the security of South Korea, which would be less provocative than a large continuing flow of new arms to South Korea, would be to place the demilitarized zone (DMZ) under effective international control in order to satisfy the South Koreans that eventual total withdrawal of U.S. forces would not open the way to surprise attack by the North. For it is this obsession with the danger of sudden attack, more than anything else, that makes it difficult for the South Korean government to accept international arrangements involving the withdrawal of U.S. forces.

Kim Il-song's proposal that both sides evacuate military personnel and installations from the DMZ is of interest in this connection.[8] Of course, North Korea would strongly oppose effective international control of the DMZ, for its basic strategy has been to end United Nations involvement in Korea and compel the withdrawal of U.S. forces, so that the two Koreas would be left to settle their problems without any form of outside intervention. Yet a U.S.–South Korean demand for international control of the DMZ to counter the North Korean demand for total withdrawal of U.S. forces would make for more balanced negotiating positions. If it became clear that acceptance of international control was the only way to achieve the total withdrawal of U.S. forces, it might seem—particularly to the Chinese and Russians—not to be too high a price to pay. In order to meet the need of both Korean governments to retain the goal of eventual reunification of Korea, the proposed agreement might contain a provision that international supervision of the DMZ could be terminated at any time at the request of *both* Korean governments.

If the North Koreans were induced to accept the concept of international supervision, they could be expected to propose as weak a form of supervision as possible—perhaps by the Neutral Nations Supervisory Commission (NNSC) or some similarly easily deadlocked body with little power to act. This would not satisfy the South Koreans, who have little respect for the NNSC and have noted how easily the United Nations observers were removed at the time of the 1967 war between Egypt and Israel. To be effective, a supervisory arrangement for the DMZ would have to have the support of the big powers, whose interests would be served by keeping the risk of war low in Korea. Theoretically, the DMZ could be patrolled by forces from the big powers themselves. Although the inclusion of both Chinese and Russian troops and the constitutional and political obstacles to the participation of Japanese forces would create extraordinary difficulties, the assumption of peace-keeping responsibilities in Korea by the big powers would have such important advantages that the possibility should not be dismissed out of hand.

If direct participation by the forces of the big powers proved impracticable, the next best choice would be for them and the two Koreas to agree on one or more other powers to provide the supervisory forces. Troops from medium-sized nations, especially from Asian countries such

8. Interview with Selig Harrison, *Washington Post*, June 1972.

as Sri Lanka, Indonesia, or Malaysia, would be suitable. A UN-sponsored body should not be ruled out, although recent trends seem to be toward disengaging the UN from the Korean peninsula: the UN General Assembly decided in the autumn of 1973 to dissolve the UN Commission for the Unification and Rehabilitation of Korea and pressures are growing for the elimination of the UN Command in Korea. If the UN were to undertake a peace-keeping mission in the DMZ, it would presumably have to be on a new basis, totally disassociated from the past UN actions on Korea that have been denounced by Pyongyang and its allies. It would probably be feasible only after both Koreas had entered the UN.

If agreement should be reached on international supervision of the DMZ and total withdrawal of U.S. forces, it should also include a provision that no foreign forces would be stationed in North Korea, in order to equalize the positions of the two Koreas.

No First Use and the International Agreements on Korea

In reaction to a proposal for international agreements concerning Korea, the Chinese might counter with a demand for no-first-use (NFU) declarations by the United States and the USSR. The Chinese have placed heavy emphasis on an NFU declaration as a first step or a parallel move toward agreements on nuclear-free zones. Whether they would make NFU declarations by the superpowers an absolute prerequisite, or would see enough advantage in the Korean nuclear-free zone proposal (especially if it might result in the total withdrawal of U.S. forces) to accept it without such preconditions, cannot be predicted. But they could be expected to press hard for the inclusion of some form of NFU pledge in a Korean nuclear-free zone agreement.

The most extreme Chinese position would be to reject the Korean nuclear-free zone arrangements unless both the United States and the USSR made global and unqualified NFU declarations comparable to the one the Chinese have made. Such a position, if adamantly maintained, would indicate that Peking saw little advantage in the Korean proposal or had little confidence it could be negotiated, or both. It would demonstrate that the Chinese placed a higher priority on an NFU pledge—either for general political purposes or as a genuine step toward arms control—than on stabilizing the Korean situation.

Although the United States would have difficulty accepting a global and unqualified NFU pledge, it could without significant risk accept an NFU declaration directly related to the Korean nuclear-free zone arrangement. For example, the United States could pledge—in consideration of the agreement by China to renounce the use of force in Korea and to respect Korea as a nuclear-free zone—not to use nuclear weapons first against Chinese territory, allies, or forces in reaction to conflict in Korea. Similarly, the Chinese could pledge—in consideration of the U.S. agreement to renounce force and respect Korea as a nuclear-free zone—not to use nuclear weapons first against U.S. territory, forces, or allies in reaction to conflict in Korea. This would mean that if the Chinese were to violate their renunciation of force in Korea, the United States would no longer be bound by its NFU declaration against China. The United States would still be restrained, however, from using nuclear weapons against China if North Korea attacked South Korea with Chinese material support but no Chinese forces were involved. The United States would not be restrained from using either conventional or nuclear weapons against North Korean forces in these circumstances, but it is difficult to imagine that American leaders might consider it necessary to resort to nuclear weapons against North Korean forces alone.

A limited agreement such as that outlined above would fall far short of the kind of NFU declaration the Chinese have demanded yet provide some assurance to them. It would at least reduce Chinese fears that the United States might launch a preemptive nuclear strike against China in retaliation for Chinese material support of the North Korean armed forces in a war in Korea. And Peking may well regard Korea as the area where conflict would be most likely to lead to U.S. use of nuclear weapons against China. Although it appears doubtful now that the Chinese would accept so limited an NFU declaration, if some of the other aspects of the Korean package attracted them, they might view a limited declaration as an entering wedge leading to other agreements that would extend its coverage. The position taken by the Chinese on no first use in relation to the proposed Korean nuclear-free zone arrangement would test whether they were willing to give serious attention to negotiating limited arms control measures or would continue to insist on relatively "pure" or "principled" positions in order to gain political or propaganda advantage.

Before countering Chinese insistence on a general NFU declaration with a proposal for a limited declaration tied to the proposed Korean agreements, the United States would have to consider the probable reaction of the USSR. No first use is not a current issue between the United States and the USSR, and to add NFU declarations to the Korean arrangements would make agreement on a Korean nuclear-free zone more, not less, difficult. Moreover, since the Soviet Union and China, although confronting each other militarily along their border, both support North Korea, bilateral NFU declarations between them relating to conflict in Korea do not make sense. The USSR is unlikely to accede to Chinese demands for a general NFU declaration, because, unlike the United States, it is subject to possible attack by Chinese conventional forces and so may feel greater need to retain the option of first use of the nuclear deterrent against China.

If the Soviet Union did not make an NFU pledge itself, what would be the effect on Moscow of an exchange of NFU pledges between the United States and China related to conflict in Korea? The Russians would probably have mixed feelings about any form of bilateral NFU agreement between the United States and China. They would be suspicious of the closer Sino-American relationship that the agreement represented and might, therefore, be less inclined to accept the other agreements in the Korean package. Another possible result might be an effort by Moscow to exploit the precedent of a U.S.–Chinese NFU pledge in order to improve the Soviet position in Europe.

The Korean Agreements as the Basis for Other Arms Control Steps

A set of international agreements containing the elements outlined above (with or without the no-first-use element) could provide a basis on which to build toward additional arms control measures in Northeast Asia. These might include agreements to limit conventional arms in Korea and expansion of the nuclear-free zone.

If the agreements worked as intended, the atmosphere in Northeast Asia would improve in several ways. First, as the two Koreas gradually adjusted to a situation in which neither could use military force to reunify the country, their rivalry would tend to shift away from the obsessive piling up of armaments and toward political activity. Second, as a result of the lowered tension in Korea, the big powers would be more relaxed about the situation there and less susceptible to pressures from the governments of the two Koreas for additional arms. Third, the reduced risk of conflict in Korea would make it harder for Japanese advocates of increased armaments or nuclear weapons to gain support.

These improvements in the political climate would increase the chances of agreement on arms control measures that now seem impracticable. One such measure might be controls on conventional arms in both Koreas. As the two Korean governments gained confidence in the reliability of the international agreements, they would perceive less need for the very large and heavily armed forces both now maintain. It might then become possible to negotiate mutual and balanced force reductions, either in manpower or in major weapons systems. The big powers might also enter into undertakings among themselves to limit the types and amounts of major weapons they would supply. The confidence of both sides in such agreements could be bolstered by provisions for verification through overflights, either by aircraft or satellites or by both.

A further possibility that might be considered if the agreements on Korea worked well is the expansion of the nuclear-free zone to include Japan. In fact, the possibility of such an expansion might be held out as an inducement to the Chinese and Russians to enter into the Korean agreements. Japan is, of course, already a nuclear-free zone by unilateral declaration of the Japanese government, and this status will be further confirmed if Japan ratifies the nonproliferation treaty. Yet China and the Soviet Union would probably like to have Japan made a nuclear-free zone by international agreement, in the same way as proposed for Korea. Acceptance of such international limitations on its freedom of action by a power like Japan, however, could hardly be expected unless the three nuclear powers agreed to important limitations on their own freedom of action in the expansion of nuclear arsenals or the deployment of nuclear weapons.

Conclusions

It is difficult to make a reasonably accurate evaluation of the feasibility of the agreements proposed, partly because of the complexity of any arrangement involving six parties, but also for lack of an adequate basis for estimating initial reactions to the proposal and the subsequent interactions once negotiations had begun. Not much has been said or written on the subject. Public discussion of the proposal, by stimulating reactions from the parties involved, would provide a more solid basis for judging what might be realistically possible.

Despite the inevitable difficulties and complexities, the proposed agreements are worth pursuing, both through further study and by sounding out the views of the states involved, for three reasons: (1) they could help reduce the danger of armed conflict in the Asian area where important interests of all four big powers most directly and obviously intersect; (2) they would provide an excellent testing ground for the reactions of the states involved to various forms of arms control; and (3) the risks involved in attempting the proposed agreements are not great and may be less than the risks involved in not attempting them.

Because of the many unknown quantities, the United States should not try initially to present a detailed proposal to the other powers. Instead, the basic ideas should be discussed, first with the South Koreans and Japanese, then with the Chinese and Russians. Discussion of the issues among private individuals in the noncommunist states should also be encouraged, which would probably provoke comment in the state-controlled press of the communist countries. It would thus become possible gradually to gain a better estimate of where each power stood on the basic points, both through official discussion and public expression of views. If this testing process showed that the ideas had a reasonable chance of being converted into international agreements, the United States could work out with Japan and South Korea specific proposals for official discussion among all the powers.

CHAPTER SEVEN

Summing Up

For the next ten years, at least, and perhaps for considerably longer, the possession of nuclear weapons will be unlikely to make China more aggressive militarily than it has been in the past. Chinese leaders will continue through this period to be preoccupied with difficult domestic problems and the potential Soviet military threat to China's borders. Furthermore, neither the trends in China's domestic and foreign policies, nor Chinese military doctrine and weapons programs, suggest that China is likely to become militarily aggressive or expansionist during this period. The principal advantages to China of its nuclear force will be that it will make the United States and the Soviet Union somewhat more cautious about risking a military clash with China, plus whatever increase in prestige attaches to being a nuclear power.

Current U.S. strategy—seeking rapprochement with China, reducing its military forces in the western Pacific, shifting to its allies more responsibility for their own defense, and defining more narrowly the contingencies in which the United States would consider intervening with its own forces—seems well suited to the situation created by the emergence of a nuclear-armed but cautious China. Prospects appear favorable for the United States to continue to downplay the military "containment" of China in favor of a dialogue aimed at finding areas of agreement with it. While this process may continue to create some uneasiness among U.S. allies, if the Chinese threat to them remains small, as it appears likely to do, it should be possible for the United States to maintain unimpaired its alliance relationships—above all the alliance with Japan, which is essential to the establishment of a more stable, less tense, international order in East Asia.

The United States should make great efforts to coordinate its policies toward China with Japan. It should also resist pressures to rely more heavily on nuclear weapons in its military strategy in Asia in order to reduce its conventional forces in the region still further, for the costs and risks of meeting a conventional attack in Asia with nuclear weapons would be extremely high.

The nuclear force that China will have within the next five to ten years will not compel the United States to make significant additions to its own existing or planned strategic or general purpose forces. The same level of strategic nuclear forces that the United States maintains to preserve the strategic balance with the Soviet Union should serve also to deter China from using or threatening to use nuclear weapons. Both the United States and the USSR, in agreeing in the Strategic Arms Limitation Talks (SALT) to rule out area antiballistic missile (ABM) systems, have concluded that effective deterrence of China will not require this costly addition to existing offensive weapons systems. As for U.S. general purpose forces, under the assumption that the possession of nuclear weapons will not increase China's propensity to attack a neighbor, the level and deployment of these forces also should not be substantially affected.

If it is true that China's nuclear force is unlikely to impose sizable new military requirements on the United States in the years just ahead, there is some merit to the argument that there is no pressing need to involve the Chinese in arms control discussions or agreements. It is not only unnecessary but probably also undesirable to include China now in the SALT negotiations, given the wide disparity between China's nuclear capability and that of the two superpowers. None of the other existing arms control agreements seems likely to be significantly impaired if China does not participate in them during the next few years. Negotiations on a comprehensive test ban or the proposed agreement banning chemical weapons can proceed without China. And there is some risk that any arms control initiatives made toward China by the United States might hinder progress in the arms control negotiations already under way with the USSR or be misunderstood by U.S. allies.

Furthermore, China's attitude toward arms control tends to discourage hopes that the Chinese might soon be drawn into serious negotiations on limited nuclear arms control measures. So long as China lacks a reliable second-strike capability and lags far behind the superpowers in the quantity and variety of weapons in its nuclear arsenal, it would be unrealistic to expect Chinese leaders to stop testing nuclear weapons.

Moreover, Chinese condemnation of most existing arms control arrangements and the sweeping nature and propagandistic tone of many Chinese arms control proposals suggest that current Chinese thinking on these issues may be on a different wavelength from the United States and the Soviet Union.

Importance of Involving China in Arms Control

Although the arguments that China is unlikely to participate in the near future in arms control agreements or negotiations and that there is no urgent need for it to do so are plausible, they are not entirely convincing. Eventually, the Chinese nuclear force will expand to the point where China will have to be included in arms control negotiations if a stable strategic nuclear balance is to be maintained in the world. The U.S. experience in engaging the Soviet Union in arms control negotiations suggests that it is not only the relative size of a nation's nuclear force that disposes it to negotiate, but also a gradual appreciation of the advantages to be gained from arms control agreements. Imaginative efforts, undertaken now, to draw China into arms control discussions should improve the prospects for Chinese involvement by the time the need for it is urgent.

Furthermore, even though China's refusal to participate in existing arms control agreements or ongoing negotiations does not appear likely to impair their effectiveness during the next few years, continued Chinese abstention would eventually tend to undermine them. Active opposition by the Chinese to existing or proposed agreements would be even more damaging. This is particularly true of the nuclear nonproliferation treaty (NPT). The Chinese are most unlikely to set out deliberately to destroy the NPT by assisting or encouraging one or more potential nuclear powers to acquire nuclear weapons, but just their continued denunciations of the treaty could strengthen opposition to it in key nonnuclear nations such as Japan. Thus, efforts should be started now to convince Peking that it would be in its own interest to lend support to, or at least to refrain from actively opposing, these arms control measures.

Trends in East Asia for the past several years have been toward declining tension and a diminished risk of large-scale war. Hostility and distrust persist in many quarters, however, and the favorable trends could readily be reversed. Some potential arms control measures, such as, for example, the establishment of a nuclear-free zone in Korea, would reinforce the movement toward a more peaceful and stable order. But no such measures could be worked out without Chinese participation—another reason why serious thought should be given to seeking to draw China into arms control discussions soon.

Arms control discussions and agreements between the United States and China could become essential elements in the long-term effort of the United States to build a new structure of peace in Asia. Discussions alone could serve to temper distrust and strengthen the détente between the two countries. The various forms of possible agreements discussed in this book could serve a number of useful purposes, including reducing the risk of accidental launching of nuclear weapons, diminishing the danger of regional military conflict that could draw in the United States and China, compelling U.S. military planners to avoid unrealistic reliance on nuclear weapons for Asian contingencies, and strengthening forces in Japan opposed to acquiring nuclear weapons. Progress toward these objectives would improve the prospects for peace and stability in Asia and thus ultimately make possible cutbacks in the U.S. armed forces in the area.

These efforts should not be discouraged by China's current rigid propaganda line on disarmament and its denunciation of specific arms control measures. There are sound reasons for believing that the Chinese are likely to become more receptive to the concept of limited arms control measures as their participation in international affairs deepens. The most dramatic evidence of this so far has been Peking's rapid transformation from a hesitant bystander, reluctant to vote on a United Nations resolution concerning the Latin American Denuclearization Treaty, to a signatory of Additional Protocol II of that treaty. In this case, persuasion, largely by representatives of developing nations whose goodwill Peking wanted, proved effective.

The Latin American nuclear-free zone is only remotely of security interest to China; Peking signed the treaty for political reasons. But there are other arms control agreements that have a direct bearing on China's security. Perhaps the most important of these is the nonproliferation treaty, which China has publicly opposed on the grounds that the aim of the treaty was to preserve the nuclear monopoly of the superpowers by preventing other nations, including China, from acquiring nuclear weapons. While it would perhaps be difficult for China to change its public position, Chinese leaders probably recognize that it would not be in China's interest for Japan and India to acquire nuclear weapons. So it is by no means impossible that persuasion by other nations might help to convince the Chinese that it is in China's own interest to tone down its public opposition to the NPT and even to give it tacit support in private.

There are a number of other existing or potential arms control measures that China could benefit from supporting. Some of these, such as the establishment of a nuclear-free zone in Korea, would diminish the danger of nuclear war in areas of vital interest to China. In fact, any form of arms control arrangement in East Asia that reduced Japanese incentives to build powerful military forces, including nuclear weapons, would offer substantial advantages to China.

A U.S.–Chinese Dialogue

The United States is in a favorable position for attempting to engage China in a dialogue on arms control. As the superpower to which the Chinese leaders have chosen, for good reasons of their own, to draw closer, the United States at present has good contacts with the Chinese leadership. The establishment of liaison offices in Peking and Washington and the appointment of distinguished diplomats to head them have greatly improved the channels of communication between the two governments. Trade has developed satisfactorily and the travel of Americans and Chinese back and forth is expanding. The atmosphere thus created appears favorable today for serious discussion of important issues. Consequently, the United States should seek opportunities to draw the Chinese into informal discussion of a variety of arms control measures, with the hope of demonstrating that it would be in China's own interest to give serious consideration to limited arms control agreements as steps along the long road that will have to be traveled before comprehensive measures such as China has proposed can be realistically considered.

An agreement on steps to reduce the danger of accidental or unauthorized launching of nuclear weapons is probably the arms control measure that can be most readily shown to be in the interest of both countries. It should appeal to the Chinese not only because of its intrinsic merit, but also because it would serve Chinese purposes to demonstrate to the Soviet Union that U.S.–Chinese relations had developed to the stage where the two countries could reach agreement in as sensitive an area as their nuclear weapons programs. Consequently, the United States would do well to open a dialogue with Peking by discussing the danger of accidental or unauthorized launch and the measures it has taken to reduce this danger. Frank discussion of this subject would benefit both parties and might lead to agreements similar to those between the United States and the Soviet Union to establish a hot line and to prevent the accidental launch of nuclear missiles. It would not be in the U.S. interest, of course, for the Russians to misconstrue or exaggerate the importance of a U.S.–Chinese agreement or discussions of this kind. Hence, the United States should take pains to convince them that such an agreement would serve Soviet interests as well as those of the United States and China.

The existing arms control agreement in which the Chinese should, perhaps, have the greatest interest—despite their past denunciation of it—is the nonproliferation treaty, but there is little chance that the United States could persuade China to adhere to it. Even though the Chinese may recognize that the treaty holds advantages for them, they would probably regard these as incidental to what has seemed to them the main purpose of the treaty—to maintain the superior position of the two superpowers in nuclear armament. Nevertheless, the Chinese may in time become receptive to discussion of the subject with the United States and less rigidly hostile to it in private than they have been in public. Even though the chances of early Chinese adherence to the treaty are probably slight, discussion of it with the United States might help to convince Peking that it is not in its interest to reiterate opposition to the treaty; and eventually, the Chinese might even come to recognize that discreet private support for the treaty would be in their interest.

It would not be fruitful for the United States to urge Peking to agree to the limited test ban treaty or to join in negotiations on a comprehensive test ban. In time the Chinese may decide that they can conduct future testing underground and be willing to sign the limited test ban, but if they do so it will be at the urging of the nonnuclear powers rather than the United States.

A U.S. No-First-Use Pledge

Some form of limited no-first-use (NFU) pledge by the United States toward China deserves serious consideration. It could have a number of important advantages: it could diminish the risks associated with nuclear weapons, lessen U.S. reliance on nuclear weapons in military planning, reduce incentives for nuclear proliferation, and enhance the prospects for drawing the Chinese into serious arms control negotiations. In taking such action, the United States would not be giving up an option of great potential value, for it is difficult to conceive of circumstances in Asia in the foreseeable future in which it would be in the U.S. interest to use nuclear weapons first. Moreover, keeping open the option of using nuclear weapons against Chinese conventional attack is of only marginal deterrent value, since China's propensity to commit its forces beyond its borders is likely to remain low, for a variety of other reasons.

The effects of a U.S. NFU pledge toward China are, admittedly, uncertain. The benefits to the United States, being long-term and intangible, are difficult to evaluate. Chinese motivations in pressing for NFU declarations by the superpowers are unclear, and one cannot be certain how the Chinese would react to a U.S. NFU initiative. The possible reactions of U.S. allies in Europe and Asia are also hard to predict, for they would be affected by the general state of the ally's relations with the United States and its attitudes toward China and the USSR at the time. Allied reactions would also be considerably influenced by the effectiveness of preparatory consultations with the United States. Possible Soviet reactions are another area of considerable uncertainty.

Reactions would vary to some extent according to the kind of NFU pledge the United States undertook. A unilateral U.S. pledge would obviously be easiest to make. It might also be less disturbing to the Soviet Union and some U.S. allies than a Sino-American agreement, for the political overtones of understanding and cooperation between the United States and China would be weaker than with a joint statement containing reciprocal obligations. On the other hand, a unilateral pledge would probably be less effective than a joint statement in improving U.S.–Chinese relations or in drawing the Chinese into other arms control negotiations. In the absence of a formal pledge, U.S. military planning and deployment could be adjusted to reflect a no-first-use position and an explanation of this offered to the Chinese. This alternative would produce significant, though lesser, benefits and would avoid some of the possible difficulties of an NFU pledge. A joint pledge by the United States and China not to use nuclear weapons against nonnuclear states would raise no security problems for either country and would probably be received favorably by U.S. allies. However, the Chinese probably would be reluctant to join in a declaration that did not incorporate a U.S. NFU pledge toward China.

More discussion of the no-first-use concept is clearly desirable before the U.S. government formulates a position on an NFU initiative toward China. Discussion could take many forms: study and debate of the issues among private arms control specialists here and abroad and publication of their conclusions; the probing of Chinese and allied views by private citizens; studies conducted within the U.S. government; and informal talks between U.S. and foreign government officials. Through such activities, a clearer view of the advantages and disadvantages of a U.S. initiative on no first use toward China could be formed. As the present discussion demonstrates, the potential advantages of a U.S. NFU pledge are important enough and the possible disadvantages tolerable enough to make it one of the most promising subjects for inclusion in a U.S.–Chinese dialogue on arms control.

Arms Control in Korea

Of the several areas on the rim of China where regional arms control arrangements might help to diminish the risk of large-scale conflict, Korea seems the most promising. It is the one area in which all four of the big powers most active in East Asia have important interests; consequently, the outbreak of conflict there would threaten to involve them. The policies of all of them toward Korea reflect recognition of this danger and a desire to avoid actions that would heighten tension in the peninsula and thus increase the risk of war.

Moreover, the trend toward détente among the big powers has sufficiently changed the political atmosphere with regard to Korea as to encourage the two Korean governments to begin a dialogue with each other. This willingness to talk, although so far productive of little in the way of concrete results, has shifted the emphasis in the policies of the two governments slightly away from military confrontation in the direction of political and diplomatic rivalry. Some form of arms control arrangement in Korea agreed to by the big powers would help to maintain the favorable momentum in and around Korea.

Because of the intensity of the hostility between the two Koreas and the deep differences between China and the Soviet Union, it probably cannot be expected that formal arms control arrangements involving the two Koreas and the four big powers could be arrived at any time soon. Nevertheless, it is worthwhile considering possible arrangements, partly in the hope that changing attitudes may make them more feasible as time passes, and partly in the expectation that active consideration by all parties concerned of ways of diminishing the risk of conflict would improve the prospects for at least tacit bilateral understandings toward this end, even if express multilateral agreements remained elusive.

The two-tier set of interlocking agreements proposed here, involving the two Korean governments and the four big powers, which would make the Korean peninsula a nuclear-free zone, obviously presents a number of difficult problems. Yet it appears to hold enough advantages for each of the parties to be worth serious consideration.

Discreet encouragement by the big powers could in time induce Seoul and Pyongyang to discover sufficient overlap in their respective proposals for a "non-aggression pact" and a "peace agreement" to enable them to enter into formal undertakings to renounce the use of force against each other and agree to make Korea a nuclear-free zone. The four big powers, jointly or separately, could then endorse the agreement between the two Koreas and pledge to respect the Korean nuclear-free zone. The United States, in order to reassure the South Koreans and also as a continuing deterrent to possible military involvement in Korea by China or the USSR, could make its pledge conditional on the continued observance by Moscow and Peking of their commitment to refrain from military intervention there.

The presence of U.S. forces in South Korea would probably become a major sticking point in any agreement such as the one proposed here. The North Koreans would press hard for total withdrawal, and they would be supported in this, though probably with considerably less conviction, by the Chinese and the Russians. Sharply differing views on this issue might conceivably be reconciled in several ways: by a U.S. agreement in principle to withdraw its forces at some undetermined date; by arrangements for the emergency return of U.S. forces as a substitute for their presence in South Korea; by an international supervisory force stationed in the DMZ; or by a combination of these measures.

Despite the difficulties involved, the concept of a multilateral agreement making Korea a nuclear-free zone should be seriously considered. While it probably would not be productive for the United States to formulate any such proposal officially in the near future, the concept deserves discussion both inside and outside the U.S. government and, informally at least, with the governments of South Korea and Japan. It could then be introduced at a later stage into an arms control dialogue between the United States and China (and discussed with the USSR as well), with the hope that China's past emphasis on nuclear-free zones and its probable interest in diminishing the danger of large-scale conflict over Korea would make it amenable to the idea.

Implications for U.S.–Japanese Relations

A central concern of the U.S. government in undertaking an arms control dialogue with China should be the effect on Japan of any agreements reached with Peking. It is essential for the United States to maintain a firm and confident relationship with Japan. Should the United States and Japan drift apart and the latter lose confidence in the U.S. defense commitment to it, there would be more danger that the Japanese, confronted by nuclear-armed potential adversaries in the USSR and China, would decide that they also must have nuclear weapons. And the emergence of Japan as a nuclear power would aggravate the arms race and make future agreements on arms control far more difficult. Therefore, the United States should seek in advance Japanese agreement in its plans for approaches to China on arms control. Most conceivable arms control arrangements between the United States and China would seem to be in the Japanese interest also. But recent experience—especially the "Nixon shock" to the Japanese resulting from the unexpected announcement of President Nixon's intention to visit China—demonstrates the extreme sensitivity of the Japanese to U.S. moves toward China and the consequent need to avoid unpleasant surprises that could damage U.S.–Japanese relations.

To be in a position to enter into significant arms control agreements with China—especially a no-first-use agreement—without undermining relations with Japan, the United States should maintain conventional forces sufficient to assure the credibility of its defense commitment. As the Chinese nuclear force expands, U.S. reliance on nuclear weapons as a possible response to a Chinese conventional attack will become less credible. Hence, the United States should move away from reliance on nuclear weapons for this purpose in its strategy and force planning and adopt the view that nuclear weapons should be regarded as deterrents to the use of nuclear weapons by others rather than as usable for responding to conventional attacks. Given current trends in U.S.–Chinese and U.S.–Japanese relations, existing and planned U.S. conventional forces appear adequate to maintain Japanese confidence in the U.S. defense commitment. If China should turn aggressive, Sino-American and Sino-Japanese relations deteriorate seriously, and the danger of military confrontation increase sharply, the United States would have to undertake a thorough review of its security policies—increasing the level of U.S. conventional forces in the region, redefining the interests it would be prepared to defend with force, or securing a greater Japanese contribution to counter possible Chinese military action. But if, as seems more likely, U.S. and Japanese relations with China should continue to improve, the level of U.S. conventional forces in or available for Asia could be further reduced.

Implications for U.S.–Soviet Relations

Maintaining the strategic balance with the USSR is, of course, of overriding importance to the security of the United States. It would be unwise to undertake any arms control initiative toward China that would endanger that balance, but there is little reason to suppose that the initiatives proposed here would have that effect. The Russians would be suspicious of U.S. efforts to reach arms control agreements with China, but this could be allayed to some extent by timely consultations with the Russians, and whatever suspicions remained could hardly be serious enough to affect major U.S.–Soviet arms control negotiations, in which both countries now have a large stake.

In fact, it is entirely possible that a U.S.–Chinese arms control dialogue would improve rather than injure prospects for successful negotiations between Washington and Moscow, since both China and the Soviet Union now seem to be seriously interested in improving relations with the United States and concerned lest the other get ahead in this respect. There are, furthermore, potential gains for the Soviet Union if a U.S.–Chinese dialogue should dispose the Chinese to consider arms control more favorably. Russians as well as Americans have an interest in inducing China not to encourage further proliferation of nuclear weapons. And a U.S.–Chinese agreement on measures to prevent conflict arising out of an accidental or unauthorized launching of a nuclear weapon would benefit the Soviet Union also and could pave the way for a similar agreement between Moscow and Peking.

Getting a Dialogue Started

One promising topic with which to initiate an official arms control dialogue with China would be an agreement to reduce the risk of accidental or unauthorized launching of nuclear weapons. It offers significant advantages to both parties and would have fewer repercussions on U.S. relations with the USSR or with U.S. allies than most other potential topics for discussion.

Many of the other possible subjects would require preparatory steps before the U.S. government could put them forward with reasonable confidence as concrete proposals. China's views on various limited arms control measures need to be probed by U.S. officials and by officials of other nations in informal discussion. The United Nations provides one good locale for such corridor conversations, which should in time provide a clearer understanding of China's developing views on arms control. Nongovernment specialists on arms control may also be able to find ways of engaging the Chinese in discussions, possibly through "Pugwash" type private meetings. In addition to seeking Chinese views, U.S. officials should discuss informally with the USSR and U.S. allies the prospects for drawing the Chinese into arms control arrangements and any problems this might raise for them.

Finally, the attitudes of China to arms control should be aired through discussions among private specialists in the United States and abroad and in published studies. Such activity should encourage the governments concerned to give greater attention to the subject and also help to elicit official and unofficial reaction to tentative proposals. This study is intended to be a contribution to that end.

APPENDIX

Chinese Nuclear Capability

Prepared by Alton H. Quanbeck and Barry M. Blechman

Intercontinental Forces

Intercontinental ballistic missiles. The program for Chinese strategic forces appears to have lost its momentum in the last year or two.[1] While the deployment of shorter-range missiles has progressed as expected, the development of the ICBM program seems to have slackened.

The Chinese apparently succeeded in designing a fusion weapon with a yield of three megatons that would be compatible with a land-based ICBM or submarine-launched ballistic missile. As of June 1974, they had conducted sixteen nuclear tests since 1964. It is estimated they now have a stockpile of two to three hundred nuclear weapons.[2]

The Chinese have produced a missile with a range of up to 3,500 miles, which could reach targets in European Russia, but this missile is not a threat to the continental United States. The Chinese are expected to develop a large, full-range ICBM that could be deployed by the mid-1980s.[3] This date represents a delay of over ten years beyond initial estimates.

In attempting to achieve an intercontinental nuclear capability the Chinese are confronted with several major technical hurdles: (1) achieving the range/payload capabilities dictated by the extremely long distances between China and U.S. urban targets (cities in the eastern United States are some 6,000 nautical miles from Chinese territory and the closest targets in the continental United States are nearly 5,000

1. *Report of the Secretary of Defense James R. Schlesinger to the Congress on the FY 1976 and Transition Budgets, FY 1977 Authorization Request and FY 1976–1980 Defense Programs* (Feb. 5, 1975; processed), p. II-16.

2. International Institute for Strategic Studies, *The Military Balance, 1974–1975* (London: IISS, 1974), p. 48.

3. *Report of Secretary of Defense James R. Schlesinger,* p. II-17.

140

nautical miles distant); (2) attaining sufficient accuracy; and (3) en-suring adequate survivability of their limited force of missiles so that it would not be an easy target for a U.S. or Soviet first strike.

These technological difficulties, together with the small supplies of fissile material available, the political drain on financial resources, and limited technological manpower, make it not inconceivable that the Chinese will defer full-range ICBM deployment indefinitely. A decision to do so most likely would be based on an assessment that the Soviet Union poses a much greater threat to Chinese security than does the United States. This would make the Chinese loath to divert resources from regional nuclear capabilities in order to build a small number of relatively vulnerable long-range missiles. While the Chinese can be expected to continue their ICBM development program as a hedge against a possible deterioration in relations with the United States, a decision to deploy the missile before the end of the decade should not be taken as a foregone conclusion.

Submarine-launched ballistic missiles. At present the Chinese have no nuclear-propelled submarines. Of the roughly forty diesel-powered submarines in the Chinese inventory, one is a G-class of Soviet design, which has ballistic missile launching tubes but no missiles. There is thus no evidence available at this time to support the view that China has any SLBM capability.

It is unlikely that China could pose a threat with SLBMs to the United States during this decade. Ballistic missile submarines would be technically more difficult and much more expensive to build than land-based missile systems; moreover, early versions of Chinese submarines would probably be quite noisy and relatively easy to detect. Consequently, a small force would be vulnerable to U.S. antisubmarine warfare forces.

Bombers. In 1972 it was concluded that the Chinese had no intercontinental bomber force and did not appear to be developing one.[4] There is no evidence that this situation has changed.

Regional Capability

Il-28 light bombers. It is estimated that the Chinese have about 200 of these aircraft,[5] which are very limited in range, speed, and payload.

4. See Secretary of Defense Melvin R. Laird, *Annual Defense Department Report, FY 1972* (January 1972; processed), p. 46.

5. *The Military Balance, 1974–1975,* p. 50.

This number probably will decline gradually. China could use these obsolete light bombers to deliver nuclear weapons—though at most one fission weapon per plane—against targets very near its borders. These bombers could be easily destroyed by modern air defense fighters or surface-to-air missiles.

TU-16 medium bombers. This is a version of the Soviet Badger that can carry a payload of 6,600 pounds to a range of 1,650 nautical miles[6] at speeds up to 590 miles per hour.[7] A TU-16 is capable of carrying three or four low-yield fission weapons, or perhaps two three-megaton bombs. Production models of this bomber were identified in China in the summer of 1970. Production was apparently suspended in 1973.[8] It is estimated that there were 100 TU-16s deployed in 1974.[9]

The range of this aircraft would enable it to reach several major Soviet cities, as well as targets in Japan, Korea, Southeast Asia, Taiwan, India, and the Philippines.[10] Its speed would give it a high probability of penetrating the air defenses of those areas, especially if the bombers flew at low altitudes within 200 miles of their targets.

Medium-range ballistic missiles. It has been estimated that by 1974 the Chinese had acquired a force of fifty operational MRBMs, with a range of up to 1,000 nautical miles.[11] These missiles would be able to cover targets in southern Russia and Japan.

Intermediate-range ballistic missiles. An IRBM, with a range of up to 2,000 nautical miles, would enable the Chinese to reach more targets further from its borders than would MRBMs. Such a weapon could hit targets in western Russia—the core of the Soviet urban and industrial base—including Moscow.

In 1972, reports attributed to officials of the U.S. State and Defense Departments indicated that the Chinese had deployed a storable liquid fuel missile with a range of 1,500–2,500 nautical miles;[12] later reports indicated that twenty to thirty missiles were already operational.[13]

6. *Annual Defense Department Report, FY 1972*, p. 46.
7. *Washington Post*, Sept. 18, 1970.
8. *Report of Secretary of Defense James R. Schlesinger*, p. II-17.
9. *The Military Balance, 1974–1975*, p. 49.
10. *Washington Post*, Sept. 18, 1970.
11. *The Military Balance, 1974–1975*, p. 46.
12. *New York Times*, Feb. 1, 1972.
13. *The Military Balance, 1974–1975*, p. 49.

There is not adequate public information at present to project how large an IRBM force the Chinese will have, or what mix of medium- and intermediate-range missiles they will eventually deploy. It is clear, however, that the longer-range weapons will constitute an important element in their strategic force.

Tactical Battlefield Systems

American analysts disagree on what Chinese policy is on the development of tactical nuclear weapons. For some time the prevailing opinion has been that it would not be in China's interest to divert scarce economic and technological resources to the development of battlefield nuclear weapons. From this perspective, it would be to China's advantage to try to limit conflicts in which it might become involved to ones requiring conventional weapons, so that its advantages in manpower resources would be decisive. Accordingly, it is believed that China would refrain from deploying tactical nuclear weapons so as to reduce the incentives for its potential adversaries to use them.

One of the earliest to deviate from this view was Alice Hsieh, a China expert, who noted in 1970 that China might already be experimenting with tactical nuclear weapons.[14] Hsieh felt that the Chinese would find such weapons promising for attacks on troop concentrations and staging areas in the event of a U.S. or Soviet invasion of China, as well as to deter the use of tactical nuclear weapons by the United States in a crisis in Korea.

In the summer of 1972, unidentified American analysts indicated that a major shift in Chinese strategy was indeed under way. They noted that the last three Chinese nuclear tests were in the ten- to thirty-kiloton range—that is, rather small weapons. They also noted that China was mass-producing a new aircraft, the F-9, at the rate of fifteen a month; this plane, it was felt, could be used to deliver the tactical weapons. Chinese stocks of the small nuclear weapons were then estimated at between fifty and one hundred.[15] This apparent shift in China's strategy was said to be motivated by the continuing buildup of Soviet troops on

14. See *ABM, MIRV, SALT, and the Nuclear Arms Race,* Hearings before the Subcommittee on Arms Control, International Law and Organization of the Senate Committee on Foreign Relations, 91 Cong. 2 sess. (1970), pp. 133–41.

15. *New York Times,* July 25, 1972.

the China–USSR border. Chinese leaders were thought to be dubious
of their ability to deter a possible Soviet attack across the border with
the small number of relatively unsophisticated intermediate-range
missiles and medium-range bombers that they could expect to deploy
before the end of the decade. The Chinese would thus consider tactical
nuclear weapons as a quick counter to the threat of a Soviet invasion.

In the absence of any official confirmation of this analysis, it cannot
be wholly accepted. A more definitive assessment will have to await
further developments.

Air Defense

Chinese defensive forces include an air defense system consisting
of early-warning and control radars, some 3,500 interceptor aircraft
(Mig-15s, 17s, 19s, and 21s), and a few hundred surface-to-air missiles
(SA-2s), mostly deployed around cities.[16] These defenses would be
relatively ineffective against low-flying bombers using modern penetration aids.

16. *United States Military Posture for FY 1974*, Statement by Admiral Thomas
H. Moorer, U.S.N., Chairman, Joint Chiefs of Staff, before the Senate Armed Services
Committee (March 28, 1973; processed), p. 27.

Bibliography

Barnett, A. Doak. "A Nuclear China and U.S. Arms Policy," *Foreign Affairs*, vol. 48 (April 1970).

———. *Uncertain Passage: China's Transition to the Post-Mao Era*. Washington: Brookings Institution, 1974.

Alexander, Archibald, and others. *The Control of Chemical and Biological Weapons*. New York: Carnegie Endowment for International Peace, 1971.

Chayes, Abram, and Jerome B. Wiesner (eds.). *ABM: An Evaluation of the Decision to Deploy an Antiballistic Missile System*. New York: Harper and Row, 1969.

Foreign Broadcast Information Service. *Daily Report: People's Republic of China* (entitled *Communist China* before August 1971); *Daily Report: Soviet Union; Daily Report: Asia and the Pacific*. Springfield, Va.: National Technical Information Service, U.S. Department of Commerce, 1963–73.

Gelber, Harry. *Nuclear Weapons and Chinese Policy*. Adelphi Papers, 99. London: International Institute for Strategic Studies, 1973.

———. "Nuclear Weapons in Chinese Strategy," *Problems of Communism*, vol. 20 (November–December 1971).

Halperin, Morton H. *China and the Bomb*. New York: Praeger, 1965.

———. *China and Nuclear Proliferation*. Chicago: University of Chicago Press, 1966.

———. *Chinese Nuclear Strategy: The Early Post-Detonation Period*. Adelphi Papers, 18. London: International Institute for Strategic Studies, 1965.

———. "A Proposal for a Ban on the First Use of Nuclear Weapons," *Journal of Arms Control*, vol. 1 (April 1963).

———. *Sino-Soviet Relations and Arms Control*. Prepared for the U.S. Arms Control and Disarmament Agency. Cambridge, Mass.: East Asian Research Center/Center for International Affairs, Harvard University, 1966.

———, and Dwight H. Perkins. *Communist China and Arms Control*. Cambridge, Mass.: East Asian Research Center/Center for International Affairs, Harvard University, 1965.

Hinton, Harold C. *Communist China in World Politics*. Boston: Houghton Mifflin, 1966.

145

Hsieh, Alice Langley. "China's Nuclear Strategy and a U.S. Anti-China ABM," in Subcommittee on Arms Control, International Law and Organization of the Senate Committee on Foreign Relations, *ABM, MIRV, SALT, and the Nuclear Arms Race.* Hearings. 91 Cong. 2 sess. Washington: Government Printing Office, 1970.

————. *Communist China and Nuclear Force.* Santa Monica, Calif.: Rand Corporation, 1963.

————. *Communist China's Evolving Military Strategy and Doctrine.* Washington: Institute for Defense Analyses, 1970.

————. *Communist China's Strategy in the Nuclear Era.* Englewood Cliffs, N.J.: Prentice-Hall, 1962.

Huck, Arthur. *The Security of China.* New York: Columbia University Press, 1970.

International Institute for Strategic Studies, *The Military Balance, 1972–1973.* London: IISS, 1972.

Jack, Homer A. "Chinese Positions on Disarmament at the United Nations," in *Disarmament Report.* Processed. SANE, the United Methodist Church, and the World Conference of Religion for Peace, March 1, 1973.

Laird, Melvin. "Statement before the Subcommittees on Department of Defense and Military Construction of the House Appropriations Committee (May 22, 1969)," in *Safeguard Antiballistic Missile System.* Hearings. 91 Cong. 2 sess. Washington: Government Printing Office, 1969.

————. *Toward a National Strategy of Realistic Deterrence.* Statement before the House Armed Services Committee of Secretary of Defense Melvin R. Laird on the FY 1972–76 Defense Program and the 1972 Defense Budget (March 9, 1971). Washington: Government Printing Office, 1971.

Moorer, Thomas H. "Statement before the House Armed Services Committee (March 28, 1973)," in *Cost Escalation in Defense Procurement Contracts and Military Posture and H.R. 6722.* Hearings, 92 Cong. 2 sess. Washington: Government Printing Office, 1973.

Owen, Henry (ed.). *The Next Phase in Foreign Policy.* Washington: Brookings Institution, 1973.

The Nonproliferation of Nuclear Weapons. Washington: Government Printing Office, 1968.

People of the World, Unite, for the Complete, Thorough, Total and Resolute Prohibition and Destruction of Nuclear Weapons. Peking: Foreign Languages Press, 1963.

Pollack, Jonathon D. "Chinese Attitudes toward Nuclear Weapons, 1964–9," *China Quarterly,* no. 50 (April–June 1972).

Quanbeck, Alton H., and Barry M. Blechman. *Strategic Forces: Issues for the Mid-Seventies.* Washington: Brookings Institution, 1973.

Ullman, Richard H. "No First Use of Nuclear Weapons," *Foreign Affairs,* vol. 50 (July 1972).

U.S. Arms Control and Disarmament Agency. *Documents on Disarmament.* Washington: Government Printing Office, 1963–73.

U.S. Congress. Joint Committee on Atomic Energy. *Impact of Chinese Com-*

munist Nuclear Weapons Progress on United States National Security. Hearings. 90 Cong. 1 sess. Washington: Government Printing Office, 1967.
————. *Nonproliferation of Nuclear Weapons.* Hearings. 89 Cong. 2 sess. Washington: Government Printing Office, 1966.

U.S. Congress. Message from the President, June 13, 1972. *The ABM Treaty and the Interim Agreement.* Washington: Government Printing Office, 1972.

U.S. Congress. Subcommittee on Arms Control, International Law and Organization of the Senate Committee on Foreign Relations. *ABM, MIRV, SALT, and the Nuclear Arms Race.* Hearings. 91 Cong. 2 sess. Washington: Government Printing Office, 1970.

U.S. Congress. Subcommittee on Asian and Pacific Affairs of the House Committee on Foreign Affairs. *United States–China Relations: A Strategy for the Future.* Hearings. 91 Cong. 2 sess. Washington: Government Printing Office, 1970.

U.S. Department of Defense. *Annual Report: FY 1973.* Washington: Government Printing Office, 1972.

Whitson, William, with Chen-hsia Huang. *The Chinese High Command: A History· of Communist Military Politics, 1927–71.* New York: Praeger, 1973.

Wriggins, Howard, and others. *India and Japan: The Emerging Balance of Power in Asia and Opportunities for Arms Control, 1970–75.* Prepared for U.S. Arms Control and Disarmament Agency. New York: South Asian Institute/East Asian Institute, Columbia University, 1971.

Wu, Yuan-li, and others. *Communist China and Arms Control.* Prepared for the U.S. Arms Control and Disarmament Agency. Stanford, Calif.: Hoover Institution on War, Revolution, and Peace, 1968.

Index